Old Testament Themes

Old Testament Themes

Victor H. Matthews

Chalice Press®

St. Louis, Missouri

© Copyright 2000 by Victor H. Matthews

All scripture quotations, unless otherwise indicated, are from the *New Revised Standard Version Bible*, copyright 1989, Division of Christian Education of the National Council of the Churches of Christ in the United States of America. Used by permission. All rights reserved

The maps on pages 6, 28, 54, and 74 are taken from Victor H. Matthews and James C. Moyer, *The Old Testament: Text and Context*, and are used by permission of Hendrickson Publishers.

Cover art and design: Grady Gunter
Art direction: Elizabeth Wright
Interior design: Wynn Younker

This book is printed on acid-free, recycled paper.

Visit Chalice Press on the World Wide Web at
www.chalicepress.com

10 9 8 7 6 5 4 3 2 1   00 01 02 03

Library of Congress Cataloging–in–Publication Data

Matthews, Victor Harold.
    Old Testament themes / by Victor H. Matthews.
        p.   cm.
    Includes bibliographical references and indexes.
    ISBN 0-8272-2712-4
    1. Bible. O.T.—Criticism, interpretation, etc.   2. Covenants—Biblical teaching. 3. Universalism—Biblical teaching. 4. Remnant (Theology)—Biblical teaching. 5. Wisdom literature—Criticism, interpretation, etc.   I. Title.
BS1199.C6 M28 2000
221.6— dc21   00-008623
                                                            CIP

Printed in the United States of America

Contents

Preface

After teaching Bible to students in a variety of settings for more than twenty years, I have come to the conclusion that they appreciate a good story but seldom see how one story may connect with others in the text. Certainly, any systematic study of the Bible reveals certain literary patterns and recurrent motifs, but to get the "big picture," it is necessary to identify major themes that appear in many of the narratives and tie characters, events, and theological positions together throughout the entire canon of scripture. It is the task of this volume to provide a "road map" of four major Old Testament/Hebrew Bible themes: covenant, universalism, remnant, and wisdom. These have been sketched out in less detail in the introductory textbook that I coauthored with James Moyer, *The Old Testament: Text and Context* (Hendrickson, 1997). In this volume I have attempted to show that these four themes comprise the literary and theological glue of the ancient Israelite writers and for those persons responsible for drawing the text into its final, canonical form.

As a way of introducing these themes and the task of this volume, let me first define each:

Covenant: This term applies to the association between Israel and Yahweh. It implies an agreement by God to provide "land and children" to the Israelites in return for their exclusive worship and obedience to the word of Yahweh. It originates in the ancestor stories of Genesis, is made more explicit through legal pronouncement in Exodus, is tied to the fortunes of the monarchy for a time, and finally forms the basis for the maturing of Israelite religion into Judaism in the postexilic and intertestamental periods.

Remnant: Because Yahweh is portrayed as a just God who strictly adheres to the stipulations of the covenant and is concerned that no righteous person be destroyed without warning of danger, the remnant theme provides that warning. God, angels, and prophets repeatedly remind the Israelites that they must obey the covenant or face God's angry retribution. These statements are designed, according to this theme, to allow the righteous to make the necessary changes or demonstrate their allegiance to Yahweh so that they will survive the inevitable destruction and form a "righteous remnant" that will rebuild the nation.

Universalism: Since they lived in a polytheistic society, it was often difficult for the Israelites to adhere to strict monotheistic beliefs. They were drawn first into henotheism, which allowed them to continue to believe that other gods existed while they chose to give their allegiance to Yahweh. Only after the exile did they fully separate themselves from the tendrils of such beliefs. The universalism theme appears to have been used to demonstrate to the Israelites why they should give their trust to Yahweh and to prove that this God is the only God. This is often accomplished by placing a statement of absolute faith in Yahweh's power as the lord of the universe in the mouth of a non-Israelite.

Wisdom: I have combined the wisdom theme with the overriding social custom of reciprocity, which forms the basis of most interactions between persons and nations in the ancient Near East. It was the task of wisdom to educate the people so that they would be aware of wise thought, wise speech, and wise action. Included in this process is the recognition of how honor and shame are tied to what is considered to be wise and foolish in ancient society.

It is my hope that this thematic approach to the biblical narrative will facilitate understanding and draw the reader more closely into the world of the Bible. Of course, these four are not the only themes that could have been discussed, and in fact I have pointed out many subthemes, motifs, and other literary devices. However, to simplify the task and, I hope, to promote more careful examination of the biblical text by my readers, I have stopped with just four major themes. In any case, I encourage the reader to enjoy the stories, but to repeatedly think, *Where have I heard that theme before?*

Introduction

Over the years many of my students have remarked that the Bible contains themes that appear to run throughout the text, tying narratives together and providing a sense of continuity. In fact, the biblical story as we know it was unknown to the ancient Israelites. They experienced the tales of Abraham, Moses, David, and Deborah in oral form. It was relatively late in the Israelites' history that a systematic attempt was made to pull these disparate stories together and form a **canon** of scriptures. Certainly, the average Israelite was aware of the ancestral stories and the law as it was developed and taught in his or her own day. But as the society grew and became more complex, the laws and the stories about the nation's origin also had to change. They were transformed to meet new situations and new understandings of God's covenant with the Israelites.

Because the biblical materials were developed, compiled, and finally written down and edited over many centuries, it is understandable that the final editors of this vast amount of material would want to insert a core message. In this volume, I have attempted to isolate and discuss four of these major themes: **covenant, remnant, universalism,** and **wisdom.** It will become clear from my frequent cross-references that these themes dovetail with each other. It invariably will happen that an episode being described in one chapter will call to mind how that situation relates to one or more of the other themes. Those that I have chosen are not the only major themes that could be discussed, but I think they are the most central. In order to touch on some additional subthemes, I have incorporated short discussions and insets within the chapters that help to illuminate these motifs and cultural traits.

In some cases it has been necessary to retrace a portion of Israelite history to explain these themes, but that is done in as brief a manner as possible. It is not the aim of this work to provide a comprehensive history of ancient Israel, and I would refer readers to the Select Bibliography for volumes that provide that type of information. However, to provide a quick reference and a sense of historical sequence, I have provided a simple guide below to some of the most frequently mentioned events, persons, and places:

Near Eastern Personal and Place Names

Babylon, a major city in central Mesopotamia on the Euphrates River, and center of empires in the eighteenth and sixth centuries B.C.E.

Cyrus, king of Persia from 559–530 B.C.E., who conquers the Neo-Babylonian empire and allows the exiles to return to their homelands

Damascus, the capital city of Syria (Aram) and chief rival to Israel from 1000–800 B.C.E.

Hammurabi, king of Babylon from 1792–1750 B.C.E., responsible for uniting Mesopotamia under his rule and issuing a law code that has many parallels with biblical law

Nebuchadnezzar, king of Babylon from 605–562 B.C.E., who captures Jerusalem in 598 and again in 587, leading to the exile of the people of Judah and the destruction of Solomon's temple

Nineveh, the capital of the Assyrian empire from 1000–612 B.C.E., located in the northeastern section of Mesopotamia, on the Tigris River

Ugarit, a Mediterranean seaport city on the coast of northern Syria that served as a trading center and "middle-man" for the Hittite empire in Anatolia and the Egyptians from 1600–1200 B.C.E.

Major Biblical Events

ca. 1000 B.C.E. United Israelite monarchy established—Saul, David, Solomon the first rulers, Jerusalem becomes the capital under David, and Solomon builds the temple

ca. 940 B.C.E. Kingdom divides into Judah in the south and Israel in the north—Jeroboam, the first king of Israel, sets up rival shrines at Dan and Bethel

722 B.C.E. Israel is conquered by the Assyrian king Sargon II and its population is deported

587 B.C.E. Jerusalem is destroyed along with the temple by Babylonian king Nebuchadnezzar, and a large percentage of the people of Judah are exiled

540 B.C.E. Cyrus of Persia conquers Babylon and allows the Israelite exiles to return to Jerusalem and rebuild their temple

I have also employed some insights from social scientific studies of traditional societies. Anthropology, sociology, and psychology are all useful in exploring the development of ancient cultures. They help to explain the context of customs, styles, and practices that seem quite foreign to us today. Although one must be careful in drawing analogies between modern ethnographic studies and ancient peoples, this is becoming an increasingly important tool, along with archaeological discoveries, in reconstructing the world of the Bible.

Note that I separate Israelite and Jewish. This is intentional, because the religion of the Israelites (1200–550 B.C.E.) was a mixture of practices and beliefs. It should be labeled *henotheism* rather than *monotheism*. The prophets are continually haranguing these people about their idolatry and their allegiance to false gods. That implies a belief in the existence of gods other than **Yahweh**. However, the official religion of the Israelites by the time of the monarchy was Yahwism, so they had chosen to worship a particular God while accepting the idea of other gods populating the universe. This is *henotheism*. *Monotheism*, the belief in a single God, did not become a tenet of Jewish belief until after 500 B.C.E. when the exilic experience had transformed the Israelite people into the Jewish people.

Aids for Using This Volume

To make this volume more reader-friendly, I have omitted the scholarly apparatus common to works for specialists, such as footnotes or other forms of documentation. I have provided a select bibliography to aid in further study and as an indication of sources that I found helpful in writing this manuscript. However, the bulk of what is written comes from my own twenty years of experience of teaching the biblical story and from numerous articles and books that I have previously published.

Throughout the volume the reader will find parenthetic references to scripture inviting him or her to make comparisons, recall previously discussed topics, or make connections. This is my way of asking you to go beyond what you find on the page. Explore the text and see what riches can be found in a more careful study of its language and stories.

As an aid to seeking out particular topics or references, an index of major subjects, as well as a scripture index, appears at the end of this book. Technical terms are placed in boldface type throughout the text, and a short glossary defining these terms is provided as an aid to comprehension.

All biblical quotations are taken from the *New Revised Standard Version.* Some quotations are taken from ancient Near Eastern texts that parallel the biblical materials. References to these works are found in the Bibliography, but they are regularly cited in the body of the text as:

ANET = J. Pritchard. *Ancient Near Eastern Texts Relating to the Old Testament,* 3d ed. Princeton, N.J.: Princeton University Press, 1969.

OTP = V. H. Matthews and D. C. Benjamin. *Old Testament Parallels: Laws and Stories from the Ancient Near East,* 2d ed. Mahwah, N.J.: Paulist Press, 1997.

The major Near Eastern texts that I will mention are:

IMPORTANT NEAR EASTERN TEXTS

Creation and Flood Epics:
Memphite Hymn to Ptah (Old Kingdom Egypt, 2575–2134 B.C.E.)
Enuma Elish (Old Babylonian, ca. eighteenth century B.C.E.)
Gilgamesh Epic (Sumerian, ca. 2500 B.C.E.)
Atrahasis Epic (Babylonian, 2000 B.C.E.)

International Treaties:
Treaty between Ramses II and Hattusilis III (Egyptian and Hittite, 1280 B.C.E.)
Vassal Treaties of Esarhaddon (Assyria, seventh century B.C.E.)

Law Codes:
Hammurabi's Code (Babylon, eighteenth century B.C.E.)
Middle Assyrian Laws (Assyria, ca. 1050 B.C.E.)

Historical Documents:
Merneptah Stele (Egypt, 1208 B.C.E.)
Mesha Stele (Moab, ninth century B.C.E.)
Annals of Sennacherib (Assyria, 701 B.C.E.)
Cyrus Cylinder (Persia, 540 B.C.E.)

Prophetic Texts and Stories of the Gods:
Balaam (Deir 'Alla, Jordan, ca. 700 B.C.E.)
Baal and Anat Epic (Ugarit, ca. 1600 B.C.E.)

Wisdom Literature:
Aqhat Epic (Ugarit, ca. 1600 B.C.E.)
Keret Legend (Ugarit, ca. 1600 B.C.E.)
Teachings of Ptah-hotep (Egypt, ca. 2500 B.C.E.)
Teachings of Amen-em-ope (Egypt, ca. 1100 B.C.E.)
Teachings of Ankhsheshonqy (Egypt, ca. 800 B.C.E.)
Teachings of Ahiqar (Assyria, eighth century B.C.E.)

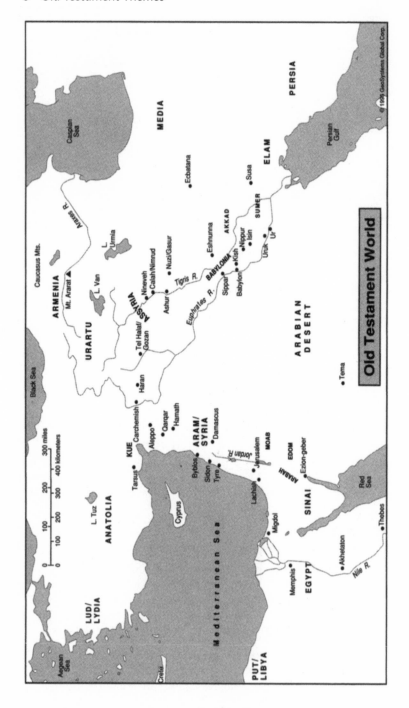

Old Testament World

CHAPTER 1

Covenant

The single most overriding theme in the Old Testament is covenant. From this all-encompassing idea flows much of the narrative, wisdom, prophecy, and spirituality of the Bible. Therefore, it is essential that the serious reader of the Bible form a clear understanding of (1) what the terms of the covenant actually are, and (2) what influences this contractual arrangement had on the development of first Israelite and then Jewish religious traditions.

In order to explore this concept as fully as possible, this chapter examines the use of the term covenant in a variety of instances in the Old Testament. First, treaty language in the ancient Near East is discussed as an introduction to contractual arrangement. The primordial narratives are also discussed briefly, and then the stipulations of the Abrahamic and Davidic covenants are outlined in detail. Finally, the expansion of the covenantal agreement, based on the growing complexity of Israelite society, is analyzed. This latter section deals with biblical law codes, the use of covenant theology in the prophets, and the importance of covenant in the postexilic development of Judaism.

Ancient Near Eastern Treaty Language

The treaties negotiated between nations in the ancient Near East are one of the major influences on covenant language in the Bible. At their heart, these agreements consisted of an oath.

7

A formal ritual, perhaps including a procession to the temple where the god dwelt, would solemnize the agreement. Both parties would recite the oath before the image of the god, and they would be honor-bound to uphold all the stipulations of the agreement. The assumption of both participants would be that the oath-breaker faced the wrath of the god for any violation of the covenant.

The earliest formal, written treaty we currently have is that signed by pharaoh Ramses II (1279–1212 B.C.E.) and the Hittite king Hattusilis III (1275–1250 B.C.E.) ten years after the inconclusive Battle of Kadesh in 1285 B.C.E. This treaty was an attempt on the part of the Hittites to balance the growing strength of the emerging Assyrian kingdom in Mesopotamia and the threat of the Sea Peoples, who were steadily migrating in larger numbers from Greece and the Mediterranean area. As a result, Hattusilis negotiated a mutual nonaggression pact with the Egyptians that (1) recognized the parity (i.e., equal power) of the two nations, (2) provided a guarantee to defend each other's country from attack, and (3) established a framework to prevent future border or legal disputes between the two nations.

Outline of Standard Treaty Format

1. Introduction: names of signatories, their titles, and sovereign powers
2. A new and official history of events leading up to the treaty signing
3. Terms of the agreement
4. A list of witnesses, human and divine, to the treaty
5. A litany of curses for violations and blessings for compliance with the treaty
6. Provisions for recording and rereading the treaty

A treaty consisted of six clauses. The opening section outlined the identity of the signatories and their respective titles and powers so that there could be no mistake about who would be held to the terms of the agreement. This was matched at the end of the treaty with a set of instructions on how to record and maintain official awareness of the treaty's terms. This could help ensure that future rulers and their administrations would maintain the peaceful relations called for in the treaty. In the body of the agreement were the provisions of the treaty. Spelled out in very careful detail would be the requirements that both sides had agreed to uphold and a statement saying that each signatory was expected to comply fully with these stipulations. A list of witnesses was affixed to the document, which included the names of the principal gods of both nations, thereby drawing the divine realm into the future maintenance of the agreement. And finally, a set of curses and blessings was appended to demonstrate the consequences of any violations and the benefits afforded to each nation for its continuous compliance.

Not all treaties were made between equally powerful nations. Vassal treaties, such as those recorded in the Annals of the Assyrian king Esarhaddon (681–669 B.C.E.), were designed to ensure the hegemony of a powerful nation or empire over neighboring states. Naturally the stipulations of such agreements, while written to give the illusion of a nonaggression pact, benefited the stronger nation at the expense of the smaller vassal states. The weaker partner was guaranteed "protection" at the cost of heavy tribute payments, a draft of young men for military and public works service, and a subordination of the vassal's culture and ability to deal with other nations.

Comparisons can be drawn between parity and vassal treaties and the biblical covenant arrangements. In the discussion below, aspects of treaty type will be pointed out and analyzed. However, it must be noted that the covenant between God and the Israelites is not a parity treaty. Once Abram accepted the covenant and subsequent generations of Israelites renewed their allegiance to it, they were bound by its stipulations and subject to punishment for violation of it. Israel thus became a vassal of **Yahweh**, unable to deal with other gods and expected to abide by the legal pronouncements given by God as clarification of the covenant agreement. Protection is promised in the form of the **"divine warrior,"** but all such guarantees are based solely on the obedience of the Israelites.

Primordial Narratives and the Covenant Promise

Within the first eleven chapters of Genesis there are at least two narratives that contain elements of covenantal or treaty language. These are the statements made by God to Adam and Eve and the promise made to Noah at the conclusion of the flood epic. Neither of these instances, however, represents a long-term covenantal relationship. Adam and Eve are given instructions (Gen. 2:16–17), which they violate, but there is no explicit commitment on God's part to do anything in return for their obedience. When they are subsequently expelled from the garden of Eden for their disobedience, God pronounces judgment on the couple, sentencing them to a mortal existence filled with pain and toil (3:13–19). However, there is no subsequent demand that they worship God; neither is there any reward offered for future obedience to God's commands.

In the case of the flood story, which will be dealt with in more detail in the chapter on the remnant theme, Noah is defined as the only "righteous" man on earth (Gen. 6:9). For this reason God is willing to make a covenant with this single individual and his family (6:18) so that they will be able to survive the catastrophe. The term *covenant*, however, is used in the form of a promise to fulfill a specific purpose. If Noah constructs the ark and follows all God's instructions, he will survive the flood. Then, at the conclusion of this natural disaster, God once again makes a covenantal promise (9:9–17). But this instance gives no hint of conditions or a continuing relationship. God promises Noah, as well as "every living creature," never to destroy the earth again by means of a flood. Admittedly, Noah does build an altar and make a thanksgiving sacrifice to God at the conclusion of the flood. However, despite the fact that Yahweh found it acceptable (a "pleasing odor"), there is no divine command for any further religious rituals (8:20–22). In fact, God never demands any form of worship from Noah or his family.

Covenant and the Ancestors

At its most fundamental, the Abrahamic covenant is an agreement first presented to the ancestor of the Israelite people by Yahweh. It is therefore a divine initiative to form an association. Abram did not seek this relationship, and nothing in the biblical text suggests why he might have been chosen. As a result, this covenant takes on additional importance because it provides the evidence of God's personal concern for humankind.

The stipulations of the covenant are intentionally simple.
• God offers Abram "land and children" and divine patronage:

> Go from your country and your kindred and your
> father's house to the land that I will show you. I
> will make of you a great nation, and I will bless
> you, and make your name great, so that you will
> be a blessing. I will bless those who bless you, and
> the one who curses you I will curse; and in you all
> the families of the earth shall be blessed. (Gen.
> 12:1–3)

Although there is no explicit command to worship Yahweh in
this statement, obedience is required to obtain the blessing and ˎ
protection offered. In that sense, this covenant fits the pattern of
• a vassal treaty, in which a stronger lord chooses his vassals to
serve him. This includes a reciprocal agreement to stand by the
vassal, ensuring both prosperity and a quick response in times
of danger.

ˏTo clarify what is at stake here for Abram, it must first be
said that he is described as an older man with a wife well past
menopause. Thus, his expectations of ever having children by
his wife Sarai seem physically impossible. He is also a man without property. His father, Terah, had taken Abram and the family
north from Ur in southern Mesopotamia to the upper reaches of
the Euphrates River and the town of Haran in northern Syria.
Even though he must leave his "father's house" (literally the
extended kinship connections in Mesopotamia), Abram is a good
choice as recipient of the covenant because he lacks what is
being offered to him.

Abram grew up in a polytheistic society. His family and everyone else he ever knew worshiped many gods and viewed the
universe as the joint creation and domain of these gods, who
represented the forces of nature. For him to set aside the worship of the Mesopotamian gods to obey and worship only one is
a truly radical idea for a person in the ancient Near East. This is
not to say that persons in Mesopotamia did not have personal
gods or patron deities. However, it would have been inconceivable and quite scandalous for anyone to worship only one god.
In fact, it would have been considered a dangerous and foolish
thing to do.

This may explain why the biblical narrative in Genesis 12 provides so few details about God's offering of the covenant arrangement and Abram's acceptance of the terms. There is no discussion, no philosophical hedging or argumentation. Abram does not even speak or make a pledge of fealty. His acceptance is noted by his departure from Haran and his arrival in Canaan at the city of Shechem. Unfortunately for modern readers, the story contains no events from the trek that must have taken Abram and his household several months. All that was important to the biblical writers was Abram's obedience. He sets a precedent for proper action when God calls.

Despite this excellent beginning, the remainder of the ancestral narrative is filled with examples of just how difficult it is for Abram and his descendants to keep the covenant. In fact, the stories of Abram/Abraham, Isaac, and Jacob/Israel are tied together by a secondary theme of endangerment to the covenant. Here are some examples of how the covenant was endangered:

Barren Wife Motif

The principal wife of each of the patriarchs is childless for a significant portion of her marriage. Sarai/Sarah is a very old woman before she conceives Isaac (Gen. 18:11), at least ninety when she gives birth (17:17). Rebekah is barren for twenty years and only conceives after Isaac prays to God on their behalf (25:21). Rachel, the favorite wife of Jacob, only becomes pregnant after suffering for several years the shame of seeing her sister-wife Leah and maidservants bear children (30:1–3, 23). Infertility in each successive generation is an unlikely coincidence, but it would be considered a disaster for the family. Having children, especially sons, was one of the most important purposes of marriage. Without a son to inherit his father's estate, the household, and in this case the covenant, would become extinct. As a result, the **motif** of the barren wife provides God the opportunity to demonstrate repeatedly the fulfillment of the covenant promise of children. It also adds suspense, leading to a climax in the narrative, as the audience waits for the birth of the next recipient of the covenant blessing.

Search for the Heir Motif

Also in each generation of the ancestors is a sense of uncertainty regarding which of the patriarch's children will be the heir to the covenant. For instance, the narrative centers on the various attempts that Abram and Sarai make to achieve their goal without God's help. Thus, Abram initially intends to adopt his nephew Lot as his heir (Gen. 12:4–5). This seems a bit odd, since God has promised Abram that he will be the father of many nations. However, his first strategy goes awry when Lot chooses to leave the promised land and settle in the area east of the Jordan, near Sodom and Gomorrah (13:11–12). Abram then proposes to adopt Eliezer of Damascus, a servant in his household (15:2–3), but God quickly sets that plan aside and reiterates the promise of children (15:4–5). Then Sarai formulates an elaborate scheme to use her Egyptian servant Hagar as a surrogate mother (16:2). Sarai offers this young woman for Abram to impregnate, knowing that any child born of this union will legally belong to her. The resulting son is named Ishmael, and Abram is extremely pleased to have produced a child, even through surrogacy (16:15).

These human measures, of course, cannot adequately fulfill the covenant promise, and God twice more will restate the fact that the now-renamed Abraham will have a son by his wife, Sarah (Gen. 17:19 and 18:10). What is proven by this multi-staged approach to obtaining an heir is that it is God's responsibility and within God's power to fulfill the covenant promise. As a result of God's intervention, Sarah conceives and gives birth to Isaac at age ninety (or ninety-one). For the biblical writer, it is the miraculous, not the mundane, that is the proof of God's promise.

The problem for the next generation begins with finding a suitable wife for the heir of the covenant. Isaac must marry a girl from within Abraham's extended family back in Mesopotamia. The patriarch insists that his trusted servant take a solemn oath in the name of "the LORD, the God of heaven and earth" (Gen. 24:2–3) that he will return to Haran and obtain a bride from Abraham's kindred. This type of marriage practice in which choice is restricted to a well-defined "insider group" is known as **endogamy**. It is employed by people who do not wish to assimilate with their neighbors (in this case the Canaanites) and who wish to ensure that their children share their own values and customs. Note that this custom continues into the third generation, when Esau is condemned for marrying local Hittite women (26:34–35) and his brother Jacob is encouraged to return to Haran to find a suitable wife (27:46–28:5).

Once a proper marriage has been arranged, however, the barren wife theme continues and is accompanied by the confusion of which child should become the heir of the covenant. Thus, when Isaac's wife Rebekah finally is able to conceive, she gives birth to twins (Gen. 25:24–26). The complications of inheritance when the cultural assumption is primogeniture (the favoring of the firstborn) then come into play. Esau, the older twin, is portrayed in the narrative as a hunter who does not concern himself with the family's flocks (25:27). He also marries two local women, thereby breaking the tradition of endogamy (marriage only within the specified group) and ignoring the wishes of his parents (26:34–35).

What is occurring in this narrative is what is known as a **disqualification story**. Because Jacob, the younger twin, would not ordinarily be able to inherit his father's property and the blessing of the covenant, it is necessary to disqualify his older brother and thus make way for Jacob to take his place. Even though this requires that Rebekah and Jacob deceive Isaac, who is now blind, the most important thing is to ensure that the right man receives the blessing (Gen. 27). Naturally, Esau is angry that his rights have been stolen from him, and this further endangers the covenant. If Esau kills his brother, Jacob, that will have a catastrophic effect on the family and will break the sequence of inheritance of the covenant promise. Thus, Jacob is sent to Haran to obtain a proper bride (28:1–2) and to escape his brother's wrath.

Now this third generation of ancestral stories continues the motif of the search for the heir as Jacob marries two sisters, Leah and Rachel (Gen. 29:16–30). Ultimately, these women and their servants, Bilhah and Zilpah, will provide Jacob with twelve sons. However, there is embedded into the narrative a contest between the sister/wives for Jacob's affection. Leah is the first to conceive, and she steadily produces a succession of sons. Rachel is barren, a clear indication that she will be the mother of the heir of the covenant. Of course, that does not prevent her from being frustrated and ashamed by her infertility (Gen. 30:1). What helps to temper this somewhat is that she is the wife whom Jacob truly loves, and Leah's frustration is evident in the names she gives to each of her sons (29:33).

When Rachel finally becomes pregnant and gives birth to Joseph, the real struggle begins to determine the heir of the covenant. He has several half-brothers who are older, and Reuben is the oldest. Thus, as in the Jacob and Esau story, a theme is created in which the younger son will surpass his brother (compare with David's rise in 1 Sam. 16:1–13). All through the narrative Rachel is described as Jacob's favorite, so indications are that Joseph will also be favored. To ensure that there is no confusion about who should be the heir, Reuben, Jacob's oldest son, will be disqualified as the potential heir because he sleeps with Jacob's **concubine** Bilhah (Gen. 35:22). This is a violation of Jacob's rights as head of the household. Bilhah has been Rachel's servant, but when Jacob impregnates her with Dan and Naphtali, she takes on the status of a lesser wife, a concubine. Reuben's misdeed, which in later periods will be construed as an attempt on the part of the son to take his father's place (see Absalom's coup in 2 Sam. 16:21–22), leaves the field open to Joseph to become the heir of the covenant.

The final step in this extended motif of the search for the heir concludes with Joseph's saga. The writers have repeatedly made the point that he is to be Jacob's heir. But to make the story that much more exciting, a dangerous twist is added. The fate of the covenant promise and the ancestral household is centered on Joseph's survival after his jealous brothers sell him as a slave (Gen. 37:28–36). Eventually the climax is reached when Joseph obtains a position as a high-ranking official in Egypt and is able to bring his entire family to that land, where they can prosper and multiply in the years to come (45:16–28).

Wife/Sister Motif

Also added to the ancestral narratives is a motif that only occurs when they enter a new land and become fearful of the local ruler. This motif appears three times (twice with Abram/

Abraham in Gen. 12 and 20 and once with Isaac in Gen. 26), and each time it involves an endangering of the covenant promise. The basic outline of the wife/sister motif is as follows:

1. Upon entering the new land, the patriarch becomes apprehensive, fearing the ruler will become enamored with his wife and kill the patriarch to obtain her,
2. the ancestral couple agree to lie, saying that the wife is actually a sister of the patriarch,
3. the ruler pays a bride price for this "sister" and takes her into his household, and
4. God intervenes to ensure that the ruler returns her to the patriarch unharmed.

The obvious danger here is that the patriarch has lost his wife and a foreigner may impregnate her. The lie is told to save the patriarch's life, but the covenant cannot be fulfilled without his wife. There is thus a serious breach of faith on the part of the ancestors, and it is left to God to provide the solution to this dilemma.

The artificial nature of this motif can be seen when it is applied to Abraham and Sarah. According to the narrative, they are both very old, and in the second instance when this motif occurs (Gen. 20:1–13), Sarah is ninety years old and may even be pregnant. Neither condition is likely to have made her particularly desirable to the local ruler. What may have happened, in fact, is the introduction of an unrelated motif into an earlier narrative. Clearly the barren wife motif takes precedence over the wife/sister motif. The latter only appears at specific points in the narrative, triggered by movement into a new land and the potential to demonstrate Yahweh's power over the god-king pharaoh in Genesis 12 and the gods of Gerar in Genesis 20 and 26.

The Sacrifice of Isaac

Part of the covenant theme is the cultural separation of the chosen people of God from other peoples and nations. Among the common religious practices of all the peoples of the ancient Near East was sacrifice. Abram had set a precedent of making sacrifices to Yahweh when he first entered Canaan. He built a crude stone altar and made a burnt sacrifice at Shechem

(Gen. 12:7), at Bethel (Gen. 12:8; 13:3–4), and at Hebron (Gen. 13:18). In this way Abram religiously staked out his claim to the promised land and officially initiated the worship of Yahweh in this place. None of this is substantially different from Canaanite practice.

Where the difference appears in religious practice is in the story of the sacrifice of Isaac in Genesis 22. There is ample evidence of human sacrifice in archaeological and textual references from Phoenicia and Syro-Palestine. The firstborn son of a family would be offered to the gods with the expectation that this would ensure future fertility for the couple. The familiarity that Abraham had with this practice may help explain his willingness to obey God's command to sacrifice Isaac. While this seems extremely illogical to modern eyes—after all, Abraham had waited his entire life for the birth of Isaac—it does fall into acceptable religious patterns in the biblical period.

Of course, the child is not sacrificed. To test Abraham's willingness to give up his most precious possession, God waits until the last possible second to call a halt to the proceedings. It could be said that Abraham passed the ultimate test of obedience to God (a stipulation of the covenant), but it should also be noted that the story provides a clear precedent against human sacrifice among the Israelites. If Abraham does not have to sacrifice his son, others need not sacrifice their sons. It could also be argued that the blood sacrifice resulting from circumcision of all male children redeems the Israelites from the need for infant sacrifice (Gen. 17:9–14).

In this story the covenant is endangered in two ways. First, if Isaac were sacrificed, the search for the heir would have to continue and the degree of miraculous intervention would have to be heightened even more considering the extreme old age of Abraham and Sarah. Second, if Abraham were to refuse to obey God's command, the covenant would be nullified as well. Thus, the narrative serves several different purposes while demonstrating once again proper behavior on Abraham's part.

The Transformation of Covenant: The Exodus and Settlement

The idea of covenant assumes an entirely new perspective with the formation of the nation of Israel. Prior to the exodus the covenant promise had been made to individuals and their families, and little in the way of ritual was required of them as an outward sign of obedience to the covenant (only circumcision in Gen. 17:9–14). Now, with the story of the escape from Egypt and the eventual settlement of the promised land, the covenant takes on a much more legalistic and political tone. At its heart, the covenant is still the promise of land and children. However, the stipulation that the Israelites must put aside all other gods and obey Yahweh alone is becoming a greater part of the narrative, sparking the creation of law codes and more complex traditions of behavior. A greater emphasis is placed on caring for one another. As the population grows, it is more difficult to maintain close relations with everyone within the community. To help manage this growing problem, the laws place a high obligation on each Israelite to deal equitably with fellow covenant partners. These new, more developed aspects of the covenant will be discussed below.

The Exodus Event

The story of the exodus event serves as a crucible out of which Israel is formed. The exodus is much like those instances in Genesis in which it appears that the covenant promise is endangered and God chooses to intervene. The burning bush **theophany** (Ex. 3:1–10), in which God speaks to Moses, takes note of the Israelites' plight in Egypt. God acknowledges the special relationship that had been established with them as the "God of Abraham…Isaac…and Jacob." In addition, there is an implicit understanding in the text that if the covenant is to be fulfilled, the Israelites must return to the promised land, where they can prosper and multiply.

The redemptive nature of the exodus event and the contest with the pharaoh simply highlights the covenant relationship. The sequence of ten plagues and the miraculous events associated with the escape across the Red Sea leave little doubt that a mighty God protects Israel. Then, during the wilderness trek to Mount Sinai, God's willingness to keep the covenant promise is demonstrated in the giving of manna and quail and the appearance of the divine warrior during the people's confrontation with the Amalekites (Ex. 17:8–13). Each of these events is designed to set God's power firmly in the minds of the Israelites (compare with the Elijah/Elisha narrative in 1 Kings 17–2 Kings 5 for a similar use of miracle stories). Each (1) demonstrates to the Israelites who really is a God, Yahweh or pharaoh, and (2) restores the sense of obligation on the part of the Israelites to obey Yahweh's command.

When the people at last reach Mount Sinai, they are presented with the implications of Yahweh's saving act: "You have seen what I did to the Egyptians, and how I bore you on eagles' wings and brought you to myself" (Ex. 19:4). Having benefited from God's willingness to renew the terms of the covenant that was made with Abraham, the Israelites are warned that compliance will require them to become a "priestly nation," enjoying the benefits of God's bounty, but at the expense of a much more rigid set of rules and expectations. In the light of this development, the covenant originally made with Abraham, which contained no explicit commands other than obedience to God's instructions, must now be quantified. The people need to know what they must do to be in compliance with the covenant and what the consequences of disobedience will be for them.

The preamble to the Ten Commandments uses the same statement of obligation: "I am the LORD your God, who brought you out of the land of Egypt" (Ex. 20:2). This reminder will precede many of God's commands from this point on and will serve as the reason why the people should obey the covenant. Their loyalty as treaty or covenant partners is now to be based on more than faith in a promise. It has a physical reality based on a formative event, and there is intimate knowledge of the power with which they have become involved.

This may be why a formal ceremony is staged to publicly give the Israelites as a whole the opportunity to reaffirm their allegiance to the covenant. Like the treaty formula described above, the **covenant renewal ceremony** functions like the clause that requires periodic recording and rereading of the stipulations of the treaty. So when Moses gathers the people at Mount Sinai, reads them the law, and then asks them whether they will comply (Ex. 24:3–8), he is following ancient Near Eastern legal precedent. He in turn is setting a precedent that will be repeated three more times during the Old Testament period.

Covenant Renewal Ceremonies

- Joshua gathers the people at Shechem to hear the law and make a sacrifice immediately after the completion of the conquest of the land. This marks the transition from the chaotic period of wilderness wanderings to the Israelites' acquisition of the promised land and is a step toward nationhood (Josh. 24:1–28; an abbreviated version appears in Josh. 8:30–35).
- With the end of Assyrian control over Judah, King Josiah initiates a reform movement that includes a covenant renewal ceremony and the resumption of the annual Passover celebration (2 Kings 23:2–3). His hope is the restoration of the Davidic kingdom and full independence for his people.
- As a means of rekindling religious fervor and obedience to the covenant, Ezra stages a covenant renewal ceremony in postexilic Jerusalem (Neh. 8:1–12). This marks the final, formal effort to redefine the covenant obligation and sets a tone for later Judaism.

The transformation of the covenant promise into legal formulas is designed to regulate social behavior and spell out religious practice and obligation. This process is the direct result of Israel's emergence as a people and their need to know what is expected of them. Although it is historically unclear when Israel became an identifiable people (based on recognition by other nations), one clue is found in the monumental inscription of the Egyptian pharaoh Merneptah (dated to ca. 1208 B.C.E.). This inscription chronicles a military campaign in which the pharaoh conquered or subdued a number of cities and groups of people in Canaan. Among the list of his triumphs is a brief mention of the people of Israel. Although this is only a snippet of information, it does indicate that the process of nation-building had begun for the Israelites by the end of the thirteenth century B.C.E. Their growing social complexity undoubtedly requires more than a "divine handshake" to ensure an understanding and obedience to the covenant.

The Decalogue

The foundation of Israel's definition of the covenant in the period from 1200–800 B.C.E. is the **Decalogue**, or Ten Commandments. This set of regulations (found in Ex. 20:3–17 and repeated in Deut. 5:7–21) provides a legal basis for Israelite social behavior. It also more clearly defines what it means to be a "priestly kingdom and a holy nation" (Ex. 19:6). In some ways these laws are unremarkable. Every people would acknowledge the necessity of legal restraints on murder, adultery, theft, and false witness as well as the need to honor one's parents. In fact, the Code of Hammurabi (eighteenth century B.C.E. Babylon) and the Middle Assyrian Law Code (eleventh century B.C.E.) both contain laws regulating such behavior.

Where the difference appears between the Decalogue and ancient Near Eastern law codes is in its demand that no other god be worshiped "before" Yahweh. In a way, this statement is not as absolute as that in the covenant made with Abraham. To say that no other gods are to take precedence over Yahweh is also a way of saying that other gods exist. Rather than being an unequivocal statement of monotheism, it is better identified as **henotheism**. This is a middle ground in which a particular god within the **pantheon** of gods is singled out for exclusive worship.

In addition, the restriction on the use of images as representations of God or as vehicles within which God is made manifest was very radical. Every other people in the ancient Near East employed idols as a part of their religious practice. Although they understood that the images began as wood, metal, or stone fashioned by a craftsman, they invented ceremonies that eventually animated the idols. For example, the "opening of the mouth" ritual in ancient Mesopotamia transformed an object into the god incarnate. As a result, service was required to show proper respect and to provide the necessities of life to the god. Food was brought regularly, and the idol was anointed and bathed as part of daily practice. It was this service to idols that was forbidden in the Decalogue. The mystery of God's appearance and the divine power that is incomprehensible to humans were maintained by the prohibition of images.

Also unique to the Israelites was the setting aside of work each week to mark the celebration of the **Sabbath**. This event, tied to God's role as the creator, was an economic absurdity. No other ancient nation was willing to sacrifice so much time to the worship of their gods. Of course, they had religious festivals and celebrations, but to completely stop commerce at least once each week would have been considered utter foolishness (see the grudging attitudes of some Israelites in Am. 8:4–5). However, it was the Sabbath that eventually became the signature event that helped to establish Jewish identity in the postexilic period (after 500 B.C.E.; see Isa. 56:1–5).

Law and the Covenant

The Israelites used the Decalogue to signal what they felt it was necessary to do to be in compliance with the covenant with Yahweh. This also set the stage for all the rest of the legal pronouncements in the Pentateuch (Genesis–Deuteronomy). The Decalogue was written as command law (**apodictic** form), whereas most of the rest of the laws in the Old Testament are written as case laws (using an "if…then" formula). The result is that the Ten Commandments functioned as foundational legal precedents upon which later legal statements were based.

Law, like society, is a dynamic phenomenon. Neither can remain static because new discoveries and inventions are always being made. New social customs develop as one people comes in contact with another. Plus, new circumstances tend to arise as a society becomes more urban-based. Thus, when the Israelite community began to settle into villages and then later into urban settings, the understanding of how law was to function also had to become more complex. For example, it was eventually necessary to go beyond just saying, "You shall not steal." In the city culture it is necessary to determine what has been stolen, how much it is worth, why a person might have committed the theft, and finally what punishment is appropriate for the crime. Individuals and judges, therefore, were continually asking the question, "But what if?" The result was that for an Israelite to be in compliance with the covenant stipulation that you must not steal required investigation, the taking of testimony, and a legal means of administering punishment.

Tracing legal development through the various periods of Israelite history reveals the growing complexity of life and the need to occasionally either modify previous legal statements or reinforce or clarify laws to ensure that they effectively protected the covenant obligations of the people. To be sure, life in a small village, where everyone knows everyone else's business, is different from life in an urban center, where only one's business associates and neighbors are familiar. In addition, the opportunities to help each other succeed in life may change as the community changes.

This may explain the repeated injunction in the **Deuteronomic Code** (Deut. 12–26), which dates to the monarchy period and the growth of urban settlements, that the Israelites were required to protect and give aid to the weak and the poor within their society. An **egalitarian** ideal is created in these passages and is best defined in the words of Deuteronomy 10:12–22. Here it is made clear that Yahweh is the supreme power in the universe, unchallenged by any other force, and yet this God has chosen the Israelites. Such a singular honor, however, requires special obligation to obey "the commandments of the LORD your God," to circumcise all sons, and to deal kindly with the "orphan…the widow…and the stranger."

Egalitarian Ideal

Yahweh is a God who "is not partial and takes no bribe …[and] executes justice for the orphan and the widow, and who loves the strangers, providing them food and clothing." (Deut. 10:17–18)

Therefore, the Israelites
- "shall also love the stranger" (Deut. 10:19)
- share the celebration of major religious festivals with "the strangers, the orphans, and widows resident in your towns" (Deut. 16:11, 14)

- leave a portion of the harvest "for the alien, the orphan, and the widow" (Deut. 24:19–21)
- will be cursed if they "deprive the alien, the orphan, and the widow of justice" (Deut. 27:19)

One example of how the law evolves and becomes more understanding of humanitarian concerns is found in the laws dealing with the treatment of debt slaves. These were persons who because of financial exigency could no longer pay their debts and found it necessary to sell themselves into temporary servitude. Laws concerning this practice appear in both Exodus 21:2–11 and Deuteronomy 15:12–18, in what are known as the **Covenant Code** (tenth century B.C.E.) and the Deuteronomic Code (sixth century B.C.E.), respectively.

Exodus 21:2–11 says that an Israelite could not be held in debt slavery for more than six years. At the end of this term, the slave could then return to full citizenship "without debt." There may have been nothing further to add to this simple statement because in the village culture it would be expected or understood that former debt slaves would need some help to get their financial lives in order after six years. However, given the changes in the world of the Deuteronomic Code (one more urban-based), the elders or royal officials might have realized that simply going back into society free of debt might not be enough to prevent an Israelite's later falling back into debt slavery. As a result, the Deuteronomic Code, which dates several centuries after the Covenant Code, adds to the original law. In Deuteronomy 15:13–14, the freed slave is not to be sent out "empty-handed." Instead, his former master is to give him an animal from the flock, grain, and wine as the basis for starting a new life. This type of legal addition is known as a codicil, and in this case it demonstrates a greater humanitarian view of the legal process.

Covenant and the Monarchy

Perhaps the greatest single factor affecting the Israelites' understanding of the covenant was the establishment of the monarchy. As is made clear in the biblical narrative up to 1 Samuel 8, Yahweh functioned as the divine king and warrior for the chosen people. When they required human leadership (Moses, Joshua, one of the Judges), it was God who raised up that individual. However, there was no sense of hereditary leadership, no continuity from one generation to the next for these temporary leaders. This lack of consistency in administration, as well as the people's desire to compete with their neighbors eventually made the monarchy a necessity. But it also required a mental transformation. The king was to be God's secular representative. It was the monarch's job to lead the army, formulate government policy, and represent the Israelites in dealings with other nations. In the process, however, God might be shouldered aside, relegated to the temple, and consulted only when there was no other choice.

In order to prevent the monarch from "outshining" God, the covenant once again stands forth as the measure of Israelite dependence on Yahweh. There are two ways of demonstrating this from the biblical text. One is the idea that the monarch serves at the pleasure of Yahweh. If the king fails to carry out his obligation to provide justice to the people and to instruct them through his example in obedience to the covenant, God has the prerogative to "tear the kingdom away" from his family and give it to another man. Although this makes the king accountable for his actions, it also introduces a degree of political instability and uncertainty for the future of the nation.

Thus, when Saul violates God's instructions to carry out a holy war (**herem**) against the Amalekites, the prophet Samuel condemns him by saying that "the LORD has torn the kingdom of Israel from you this very day, and has given it to a neighbor of yours" (1 Sam. 15:28). Similarly, when Jeroboam, the first king of the Northern Kingdom of Israel, engages in a series of **cultic** violations by building alternative worship centers at Dan and Bethel and placing a golden calf in each, the prophet Ahijah is sent to tell him that Yahweh "will bring evil upon the house of Jeroboam" and "cut off from Jeroboam every male" (1 Kings 14:10).

The second way in which the covenant is invoked to manage the activities of the monarchy is in the special relationship that is established with the house of David. When David purposes to construct a temple to house the **ark of the covenant,** his court prophet Nathan tells him that God does not require such a dwelling (2 Sam. 7:2–7). However, God has chosen to strengthen David's "house" by firmly endorsing it as the ruling dynasty in Jerusalem. This enhanced contractual arrangement or covenant is both a reiteration of the covenant made with Abraham and a codicil or additional stipulation. Like Abraham's covenant, the covenant made with David's "house" involves elements of a vassal treaty—land and protection. However, unlike the original situation with Abraham, it is assumed that an agreement already exists between these parties based on God's previous services rendered to the king and to the nation:

> I took you from the pasture, from following the sheep to be prince over my people Israel; and I have been with you wherever you went, and have cut off all your enemies from before you; and I will make for you a great name, like the name of the great ones of the earth. And I will appoint a place for my people Israel and will plant them, so that they may live in their own place, and be disturbed no more; and evildoers shall afflict them no more, as formerly, from the time that I appointed judges over my people Israel; and I will give you rest from all your enemies. (2 Sam. 7:8–11a)

David's covenant hinges on a repetition of God's promise of a "place" for the people of Israel (2 Sam. 7–10), as well as the new promise of the maintenance of the king's dynasty. These operate similarly to Abraham's covenant, which was based on a promise that he would become "a great nation" and a blessing to all the families of the earth (Gen. 12:2–3).

Most important politically, David is assured that his son will rule after him and that his descendants will continue to rule the kingdom "forever." At first glance, this statement sounds a good deal like the promise made to Abraham that he would be the "father of many nations." The difference comes in when David's descendants inevitably fail to be just and they commit crimes that violate the Abrahamic covenant and the Ten Commandments. At that point, they, as individuals, are punished.

However, the dynasty lives on, and God's "steadfast love" or "faithfulness" (Hebrew *hesed*) is not withdrawn (2 Sam. 7:12–16). The result is a lessening of the dangers over succession and a sense of "divine right" to rule.

The key word in this promise is *hesed*. It is a technical, legal term that appears in covenant statements throughout the Bible. A psalmist or a prophet can impress on his or her audience that what is being said is in reference to God's covenant relationship by using *hesed* (see the refrain in Ps. 136; Hos. 6:6). This relationship is everlasting, based on God's mercy and concern for Israel. In the context of David's house, it is a reassurance of continual direction and a seal of divine approval for this dynasty's rule. When Solomon succeeds his father, David, on the throne, the promise to Abraham and to David seems to have been fulfilled:

God to Abraham after the patriarch agrees to sacrifice Isaac: "I will indeed bless you, and I will make your offspring as numerous as the stars of heaven and as the sand that is on the seashore. And your offspring shall possess the gate of their enemies." (Gen. 22:17)

Summary of the covenantal promise in Solomon's time: Judah and Israel were as numerous as the sand by the sea; they ate and drank and were happy. (1 Kings 4:20)

Such idealized statements, however, have the ring of political propaganda rather than divine fulfillment. Very soon adjustments would have to be made to fit changing political realities.

What is also curious about the two approaches to the monarchy in the biblical narrative is the way in which they appear to operate side by side throughout the history of the monarchy. Once the nation divides into two kingdoms, Israel and Judah, the idea of covenant is also divided. According to the official records contained in the book of Kings, Judah and Jerusalem continue to adhere to the Davidic dynasty, and presumably this four-hundred-year period of political stability is based on God's covenant with David. Assassination and the overthrow of kings occur only a couple of times in Judah (2 Kings 14:19; 21:23).

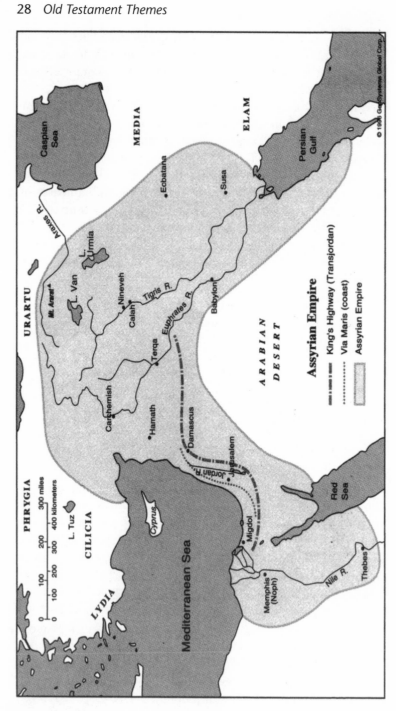

On the other hand, the Northern Kingdom of Israel is continually troubled by political turmoil. Because its leaders lack divine right in the form of a direct covenant statement from God, there is more opportunity for political adventurism. The rule in Israel becomes "succession by assassination," with one military coup d'etat after another. The only legitimating factor in this process is the occasional intervention by God's prophet, designating who should be the next king (see 2 Kings 9:1–13). The apparent result is divine sanction for rebellion and civil war. Such a system must inevitably undermine the authority of the monarchy and is a prime factor in the conquest and destruction of the Northern Kingdom.

The Role of Prophets and the Covenant

It is possible that there would not have been any prophets if the people and their leaders had not been violating the covenant. The prophets' task was to remind the people of the stipulations of the covenant. This is again a part of the ancient Near Eastern treaty formula that required periodic rereading of the agreement so that each successive generation would be aware of its obligations under the covenant. It also touched on the fact that the covenant was made with God, and, therefore, the people could expect to face the righteous judgment of Yahweh when they failed to keep the covenant. The punishments predicted by the prophets are in line with the section on curses and blessings found in ancient treaty documents.

One way that the prophets demonstrated God's concern over the covenantal failures of kings and priests was through public pronouncement and enacted or dramatized prophecy. So we find Elijah challenging the introduction of Baal worship in Israel by calling on the prophets of that Canaanite god to meet him for a cultic showdown on Mount Carmel (1 Kings 18). The theatrics involved in this public confrontation are designed in the most graphic way possible to demonstrate the power of Yahweh and, therefore, to convince the people to realign their allegiance to the God of the covenant.

In a similar vein, Amos, a farmer from Tekoa in Judah, travels north to Bethel and speaks at the royal shrine in that Northern Kingdom city. His message is quite simple: "Seek the Lord and live" (Am. 5:6). Covenant theology is thus boiled down to its lowest common denominator. Once again the people are reminded of their promise to worship only Yahweh and to obey the law. Amos particularly emphasizes the Israelites' failure to meet their obligation to care for the poor and weak, condemning those "who trample the head of the poor into the dust of the earth" (Am. 2:7; see also Am. 5:11; 8:4). This violates the egalitarian ideal that maintains that all Israelites are equal under the law and that the weak should be championed, not oppressed by the wealthy and powerful.

Another type of prophetic "display" can be found in the marriage between the prophet Hosea and a woman named Gomer, who subsequently commits adultery against her husband (Hos. 1–3). This marriage becomes a metaphor for the unfaithfulness of Israel, and Gomer's adultery is synonymous with the idolatry of the Israelites who rely on the Canaanite gods rather than Yahweh. The marriage contract in this **enacted prophecy** makes an excellent parallel with the covenant.

To further illustrate just how serious conditions had become in Israel, the prophet Hosea names his third child *Lo-ammi,* "Not My People," a repudiation by God of Israel's position as a covenant partner (Hos. 1:9). The people had moved so far away from the stipulations of the agreement with Yahweh that the prophet can compare their love *(hesed)* to "the dew that goes away early" (Hos. 6:4). But it is this *hesed,* the technical term for love or mercy, that is the basis for the covenant in the first place. It is this "steadfast love" that God desires, not sacrifice or other empty rituals (Hos. 6:6).

Isaiah also spars with kings as he champions God's role as covenant partner. During one of the most difficult periods of Judah's political life, the Syro-Ephraimitic War (730s B.C.E.), Isaiah confronts King Ahaz and tells him to do nothing but have faith in the divine warrior, despite the imminent invasion of the country by hostile forces from Israel and Syria (Isa. 7:4–9). This was too much for any political leader to bear. How could he in good conscience stand aside during a time of crisis? Isaiah offers him proof in the form of a sign, but the very practical-minded king refuses to "put the LORD to the test" (7:12). Ahaz's refusal, however, provides the opportunity for the prophet to issue an **annunciation** statement, predicting the birth of a child and the quick extinction of the physical threat to Judah. Even the child's name, Immanuel, "God is with us," is a graphic indicator of who is responsible for these events. But there is also a sense of desperation because the child's short transition from infant to adult is actually to be the measure of how long it will take for Judah's enemies to be destroyed and Judah to be impoverished (Isa. 7:14–25).

Covenant and the End of the Monarchy

The destruction of the Northern Kingdom of Israel in 722 B.C.E. by the Assyrian empire shattered many Israelites' concept of the covenant with Yahweh. They had become complacent, assuming that the cycle of sin, repentance, and restoration (as it had occurred throughout their history) would always continue. The warnings of prophets like Amos and Hosea had fallen on deaf ears. The call to return to the covenant (Am. 5:4–6) and abandon meaningless ritual and social abuses (Am. 5:21–24; 8:4–6) had no significant effect.

Thus, when Samaria is captured (722 B.C.E.) and a large portion of the population is deported, the meaning of life is lost for many of the people. It is likely that some in the Southern Kingdom of Judah, of course, saw this as Israel's "just deserts." However, this self-serving moralizing did not preserve Judah from also being overrun by Assyrian armies and then being torn apart during the seventh century by the struggle between Egypt and Babylon for supremacy in the fertile crescent. Prophets had to go to extreme lengths to prevent even further destruction. Casting himself in the role of a slave or a prisoner, Isaiah sought to convince King Hezekiah not to join a rebellion led by the Philistine city of Ashdod in 711 B.C.E. (Isa. 20). To do this, the prophet walked around naked to illustrate the fate of those who revolted against Assyria, "the rod of my [God's] anger" (10:5).

As Judah was squeezed between the political ambitions of Egypt and the emergent Mesopotamian empire of the Babylonians, the prophets time and again laid before the people the proposition that their fate was a direct consequence of their violation of the covenant with Yahweh. During the midst of the Assyrian invasion of Judah, the prophet Micah tells the people that "all this is for the transgression of Jacob and for the sins of the house of Israel" (Mic. 1:5). In his zeal to return the nation to the covenant, Micah condemns Jerusalem and Samaria as the source of social infection and religious corruption. For him and many rural inhabitants of Judah, the way to redemption was to return to a simpler existence in which obedience to the covenant meant that they were "to do justice, and to love kindness *[hesed]*, and to walk humbly with...God" (6:8b).

Echoing Micah's sentiments, Jeremiah's "Temple Sermon" is one of the best examples of prophetic rhetoric (Jer. 7 and 26). Standing in the doorway of the Jerusalem temple on a feast day, the prophet condemned the building that had become an idol unto itself. He tells the people that it is up to them to allow God to "dwell with you in this place" (Jer. 7:3). Jeremiah recites the terms of the covenant, in the form of the Ten Commandments. He then assures his audience that they cannot violate each and every one of them "and then come and stand before me [God] in this house, which is called by my name, and say 'We are safe!'" (7:10).

Despite the prophets' warnings, eventually, in 587 B.C.E., Jerusalem also fell. The temple and most of the city were destroyed and many of the people were taken into exile in Mesopotamia. All of the institutions that they had created (monarchy, capital city, temple) had been taken away from them. The prophets, like Ezekiel, spoke of an eventual restoration and return, but for the next several generations, the people of Judah would live as exiles. Curiously, what they still had was the covenant promise, freed from the overlay obscuring it since the establishment of the monarchy. It was the job of the prophets and the people themselves to refocus their identity and culture on being the people of the covenant.

To cope with the situation presented by the exile, the prophets further developed the concept of **theodicy**, a rationalization of events based on God's plan for the people. The prophets, however, had to explain why God had in fact punished the nation with such utter destruction, and they had to offer hope that eventually the people would be allowed to return and rebuild their land. Thus, despite the common belief that when a nation is defeated, its gods are also defeated, the prophets argued that God had not failed or been defeated by the gods of the conquering nations. And, most importantly, the covenant promise was still intact. It was simply necessary for the people to once again undergo a period of purification (see the wilderness theme in chapter 2). Once this was completed, they achieved a new understanding of God and themselves, which made it possible for the covenant to be fulfilled.

It was the words of Jeremiah and Ezekiel during the time when the people of Judah were taken into exile that set the tone for the transition to a new understanding of the covenant. Even at the moment when the exiles were being driven from their homes, the prophets spoke of eventual return. Jeremiah told them that God would one day "gather them from all the lands" where God's anger and indignation had cast them, and they would be brought back to Palestine where they could live in safety (Jer. 32:37). Similarly, Ezekiel, from his vantage point as a member of the exilic community in Mesopotamia, proclaims that Yahweh "will take you from the nations,…and bring you into your own land" (Ezek. 36:24). Once this longed-for restoration occurs, God will then transform the people, giving them "a new heart" and "a new spirit" (Ezek. 36:26), or "one heart and one way" (Jer. 32:39), so that their "fear" of God forms the basis for continual obedience. A true "everlasting covenant" can then be made with them, and God will be able to "rejoice in doing good to them" (Jer. 32:40–41).

Postexilic Concepts of Covenant

The actual experience of the exile, lasting sixty years (598–538 B.C.E.), did serve as a crucible of change for the people of the covenant. Some undoubtedly chose to join the "winning side" and were assimilated into the Babylonian population. For those who wished to hold on to their heritage, some hard decisions had to be made. As the generation that had come into exile passed from the scene, it must have become evident to the people that they had to create for themselves a distinct cultural identity, or they would simply be absorbed into that of their Babylonian neighbors. It was from this realization that the Jewish Identity Movement was born and the development of Judaism as a unique religion and cultural phenomenon took its origin.

Unfortunately, the biblical text does not tell us very much about the activities of the exilic community. One can only infer what took place, based on the issues raised and attitudes expressed by prophetic voices after the exile (Haggai, Zechariah, Malachi) and the administrative policies of Ezra and Nehemiah (both dating to the late fifth century B.C.E.). However, it seems clear that the leadership, whoever they may have been (Ezekiel does mention the "elders of Judah" in Ezek. 8:1), began the task of identifying those values and institutions that the exiles wished to use to create their identity as a people. The chart below outlines those that were most emphasized:

Elements of the Jewish Identity Movement

1. **Development of a canon of scriptures**
   This entailed the gathering of manuscripts, the determination of those documents considered to be essential to an understanding of the origins of the nation and of the covenantal agreement with God, and the initiation of an editing process to create a standard version (not completed until the first century C.E.). This also included the decision to retain Hebrew as the liturgical language of religion and ritual even though it was no longer the spoken language of the people. Evidence of the early development of the **canon** can be found in the prologue of the second-century **Deuterocanonical** book of Sirach (Ecclesiasticus) in which the sage Jesus Ben Sira lists the traditional divisions of the canon: "the Law and the Prophets and the others."

2. **Endogamy**
   Intermarriage was considered a danger to the exilic community's distinct identity and therefore was banned. This helped to ensure that children were trained in a single religious and cultural tradition by both parents. Couples would not have to make the decision to follow the religion of one or the other spouse. This also ensured that inheritance of property and inheritance rights were retained by the exilic community. Evidence for this practice in the postexilic

period can be found in the reforms instituted by Nehemiah (10:30 and 13:23–30) and Ezra (9—10:17). Both these men, appointed by the Persian king to administrate and bring order to the Persian province of Yehuda, enforced endogamy on the returned exiles in Judea. This was presumably because a ban on mixed marriages was the norm in the diasporic Jewish community.

3. **Sabbath Worship**
   The recognition of Yahweh as the only God in the universe was publicly professed through the weekly celebration of creation in the Sabbath ritual. This was a family-based form of worship and did not require temple, priest, or other intermediary (note that in the list of festivals in Lev. 23:1–8, reference to priests and the public cult are omitted). As such, it was the perfect solution to the exiles' need for religious ritual in a place where they lacked the ecclesiastical structures and personnel that had existed in Jerusalem. Even after the rebuilding of the Jerusalem temple, the postexilic voice of Isaiah (56:2–8) classifies the observance of the Sabbath as the key to membership in the covenant community. Sabbath worship also took the place of animal sacrifice, replacing one form of economic gift with another. By giving up one seventh of their work time each week, the exiles demonstrated a remarkable allegiance to their God. In the late fifth century, Nehemiah legislated the Sabbath in Jerusalem when it was being neglected or abused by greedy farmers and merchants (Neh. 10:31; 13:15–22).

4. **Ritual Purity**
   Starting with the creedal statement in Exodus 19:4–6, the people of the covenant were told by God that they were set aside from other nations and were to become a "priestly kingdom and a holy nation." As a means of outwardly demonstrating this condition, additional laws, in the form of the **Holiness Code** in Leviticus (chaps. 17—26) and other priestly legislation

(Lev. 1—16, 27; Num. 1—10), placed new restrictions on the people. Most especially, they were to seek to be ritually "clean" and avoid that which was "unclean." Dietary restrictions, prohibitions against certain mixtures (fabrics, seeds, crossbreeding, plow animals), and ritual bathing became cultural norms.

5. **Circumcision**
   This initiation ritual (first mentioned in Gen. 17:9–14) is reemphasized as a mark of membership in the covenantal community for males. The procedure is a form of ritual scarring and a sacrificial act since blood is shed. Accompanying the act is the pejorative labeling of the "uncircumcised" as outside the "chosen people" (Isa. 52:1; Ezek. 44:9).

Armed with this cultural arsenal, it was possible for a people who could now be referred to as Jews to survive the exile and prepare to face a future based on a common heritage. It also eliminated the need, in many of their minds, to return to Palestine. Although the prophets had reiterated the divine promise of a restored community that would find its way back to Palestine, not all the exiles were committed to the idea that they had to return to Palestine and restore Jerusalem and the temple to be obedient to their covenant obligations. Jeremiah had told them in a letter that they were to settle into their new circumstances in the exile. They were to "build houses...plant gardens...take wives...multiply there...and pray to the Lord" for the welfare of their new land as well as themselves (Jer. 29:5–7).

Thus, even at the moment (ca. 538 B.C.E.) when Isaiah's voice from the exile began to proclaim that Israel "has served her term" and that her "penalty is paid" (Isa. 40:2), the understanding of what it meant to be a part of the covenant community became a matter of dispute again. Cyrus, the king of Persia, gave the exiles the opportunity to return to their homeland and to rebuild the temple to their God. However, not every exile wished to return. Many, if not most, chose to remain in Mesopotamia and Egypt, where they had established lives, businesses, and associations. They saw no abiding reason for leaving this all behind. After all, the prophet Jeremiah had told them that Yahweh could be worshiped in any land (Jer. 29:7, 12–13). Of course, he had also said that God would restore the nation and "fulfill to you my promise and bring you back to this place" (29:10). But it was felt by many that the promise could be kept wherever the people found themselves.

Those who did choose to return to Jerusalem did not share these feelings, or they had a vested interest in a return to Palestine. For those who listened to Isaiah's proclamation of release, the only way in which the covenant promise of land and children could be fulfilled was in their retaking the promised land. In that way, "the glory of the Lord" could be revealed, displaying the evidence of God's incomparability to all other gods (see Isa. 40:12–31). In this way, they would be able to restore the land once again as the place where God's name dwells and to restore their identity as people of the covenant.

The exiles who returned from Mesopotamia in a succession of waves over a hundred-year period had to cope with the physical problems of rebuilding as well as the social problems associated with restoring their sense of identity. The land was in ruins. Its fields and vineyards had, in many cases, lain fallow for decades and would require huge amounts of labor and funds to bring them back into production. Jerusalem, although it probably had some inhabitants, lacked defensive walls, and its prestige was only a memory.

Nearly a generation passed before the temple was rebuilt (in 515 B.C.E.), and that was simply because there were too many other, more immediate concerns to be met. Prophets like Haggai and Zechariah rebuked the people over this failure. Haggai reminded the returnees and their leader Zerubbabel that God would not fulfill the covenant promise of fertility for the land while they neglected the house of the Lord (Hag. 1:7–11). Once the temple was rebuilt, with the aid of the Persian king Darius, a cultural split occurred between those who had returned and those who chose to stay in exile. With the monarchy extinguished, the priestly community was not only restored to power but also functioned as the sole voice of religious authority to the people of the Persian province of Yehuda.

As a result, new interpretations and accommodations were made to the law that had been formulated during the exile. For instance, in many cases intermarriage occurred for economic reasons. It speeded up the restoration of the land through combining established farmland with undeveloped acres and provided the capital needed to establish businesses or expand households. This secularized attitude toward one of the tenets of the Jewish Identity Movement most likely explains why Nehemiah and Ezra, coming from the diasporic community, were so upset by what they found when they returned to Jerusalem in the late fifth century. Their understanding of the covenant and of Judaism had become static, set in traditional terms that were not supposed to be changed or violated. Although they were temporarily able to impose their will on Jerusalem, it did not last, and the result was the development of variant Jewish traditions in Palestine and in the **diaspora**.

Ultimately, however, what remained for both the **diasporic community** and the returnees was the covenant promise. It functioned as a social contract as well as social glue for their communities. The promise of "land and children" for the majority is therefore transformed. Having a "promised land" no longer meant simply Canaan/Palestine/Israel. Rather, it was broadened to mean wherever they lived as members of the covenant community. Further, the promise of "children," as it always did, betokens God's concern for them and the granting of those needs that hold them together as a people.

CHAPTER 2

Remnant

Implicit in the ancient Israelites' basic understanding of their God was the idea of justice. Like the Mesopotamian and Egyptian gods with which they were familiar, Yahweh established the rules of nature and of humankind. However, the gods of the polytheistic cultures were amoral in character. They represented the forces of nature (from watery chaos to life-giving sunshine and rain) and as such were often unpredictable. Of course, the ancients could discern the regular changes in the seasons and the climatic patterns that brought rain to help them plant their fields and grow their food. However, when a break occurred in these patterns, and either a drought or a flood occurred, they were baffled as to why the gods would allow such things to happen. Sacrifices were made to propitiate the angry gods, but there were no guarantees. This may explain why the gods in Mesopotamian epics so often are portrayed as spoiled children, tricksters, and unthinking and belligerent entities.

In contrast, the Israelites portrayed their God as a judge, who weighed the actions of the chosen people against the covenant obligations that they had agreed to obey. Righteousness meant obedience to the law given to them by God. And God was also considered to be righteous because of the consistency of action and basic morality displayed in all Yahweh's dealings with the Israelites and other nations. With a basic standard in place, however, came the understanding that there were consequences for inappropriate or covenant-breaking behavior. A "just god," like the "just king" of the monarchy period, administered the people as a father or mother cared for children. This included both rewards (land and children, according to the covenant promise of Gen. 12:1–3) and punishments (drought, famine, plague, and war).

Given the fact that no human is perfect, the Israelites understood that they could expect periodic punishment. But, like children, they also hoped to either lessen its severity or to convince God that they had learned their lesson and could be trusted to return to the true path without the use of corporal punishment. This latter hope was seldom realized since, like the maxim in the Assyrian sage Ahiqar's writings, God apparently believed in the principle, "spare the rod, spoil the child."

How, then, was Israel able to withstand the agricultural disasters so common to the Palestine area (lower-than-average rainfall one out of every three years) and the devastation of war as rampaging armies burned and looted their way through the nation? The answer comes in the development of theodicy, a rationalization for God's actions based on the principle of justice and human failings. Like their neighbors (see the Moabite document below), the Israelites understood that God could become angry and allow them to suffer when they failed to obey the law or were not continuous in their devotion to worship. These violations brought swift action against them, and at times the punishment was so severe that the fate of the entire nation was at risk.

> Omri, ruler of Israel, invaded Moab year after year because Chemosh, the divine patron of Moab, was angry with his people. ("Mesha Inscription," *OTP*, p. 158)

The biblical narrative includes many instances in which it had become clear that drastic measures had to be taken to save the people from their corruption. In some cases, this meant the execution of a lawbreaker and his family (see the punishment of Achan in Josh. 7) to remove any further contagion. However, in more dangerous situations, the entire nation or even the entire world could be at risk of God's wrath. Although the divinely planned punishment fit the crime, it also had the potential to remove all life from the planet. What preserves humanity and also provides a model of restoration and rehabilitation is the **remnant** theme.

Characteristics of the Remnant Theme

- A just God must act morally
- It would be immoral to destroy the righteous without sufficient warning
- A divine warning is always provided so that the righteous can prove themselves worthy of survival
- The surviving remnant, now purified by the destructive event, are the core from which the nation is restored

The remnant theme is centered on the principle that God is a moral and just being. As such, it would be inconceivable that Yahweh would destroy both the righteous and the unfaithful without first warning them of the danger with which they are faced. This warning might come from God or, more usually, from a messenger (angel) or representative of God (prophet). It is then up to the audience of this message to take steps to ensure their preservation. In this way, the truly righteous demonstrate that they are God's true people and therefore worthy to survive the punishment. Once God has completed the destructive act aimed at eliminating the corrupt elements in the nation or the world, the righteous remnant stands forth as the seed from which the covenantal community is restored. They have been purified in the crucible of destruction, whatever form it may have taken, and are therefore more likely to remain faithful to God's word.

In the remainder of this chapter, examples of the remnant theme will be discussed in detail. Although there is a greater complexity to some of these stories, they all center on the basic characteristics outlined above.

Noah and the Flood

The biblical flood epic is a compilation of at least two versions of the story that have been woven together to form a reasonably coherent tale. There are a few inconsistencies (the number of animals placed in the ark), but it is clear that an underlying outline drives the narrative forward. It is also possible to state that the biblical writers were aware of more ancient versions of this story that had been composed in Mesopotamia (Atrahasis Epic and Gilgamesh Epic). As is so often the case, the biblical writers drew from the wider cultural milieu of the ancient Near East but then placed their distinctive theological stamp on the materials to demonstrate the power and supremacy of Yahweh.

The story of Noah and the flood begins with a difficult passage describing the licentious activities of the "sons of God" (Gen. 6:1–4). This is apparently a fragment from another epic tale and may or may not have had anything to do with the Noah story. However, its placement here does bolster the statement in verse 5 that God is angered by the "wickedness of humankind." In this way, the flood story takes on an aspect of a morality play in which humanity brings on itself a deserving punishment. It also stands in stark contrast to the Mesopotamian flood epics that either provided no explanation for why the gods inflicted the flood on the world (Gilgamesh) or simply blamed it on the noise made by humans that angered the gods (Atrahasis). There is no sense of justice in the Mesopotamian versions because these people tended to think of their gods as forces of nature that could not be controlled, only endured.

> Anu the godfather, Enlil, and Ninurta convened the **divine assembly**, which decided to flood the earth. (Gilgamesh, *OTP*, p. 26)
>
> In less than 1,200 years…there were more and more workers in the land…The uproar disturbed the divine assembly. When Enlil heard the noise, he complained: "I cannot stand this uproar, I cannot sleep." (Atrahasis, *OTP*, p. 35)

Following the pattern of the remnant theme, God acknowledges Noah's righteousness (6:8–9) and provides him a warning of the coming catastrophe. Embedded in the word of destruction are also the specifications for survival, if Noah chooses to follow them. Throughout the story the caring nature of God is repeatedly displayed. Yahweh speaks directly to Noah, gives him exact dimensions for his ark, and makes it clear what must be done to save the animal species of the earth (6:14–21).

The building of the ark is also a component in the Gilgamesh Epic. However, the hero of that story, Utnapishtim, only learns of the danger indirectly as one of the gods speaks to the wall of his hut. In addition the dimensions of his craft are in the form of a perfect geometric shape (a cube) and are designed to provide magical protection for the occupants. Noah's vessel will have God's protection and thus does not require any other aid. In fact, when the flood begins, God shuts the hatches of Noah's ark (7:16), whereas Utnapishtim himself has to make his craft secure.

To demonstrate that Noah is in fact worthy of survival, the biblical narrative repeatedly states that he was "blameless in his generation" (6:9) and "did all that God commanded him" (6:22; 7:5). He builds the ark, gathers the specified animals, brings his family with him into the ark, and trusts in God's protection during the flood. In this way, he secures the right to be a part of the remnant that will ensure that life on earth, as it was originally created, will endure and restore itself.

Marking the resolution of the story is the sacrifice made by Noah once the waters of the flood have subsided. This scene is also found in the Gilgamesh Epic, but again with a major difference. Noah performs an act of thanksgiving that is acknowledged as "pleasing" by God (8:20–21). As a result, God promises never again to destroy the rhythm of nature in this way and then renews the covenant of fertility that was first established with Adam (Gen. 1:28–30). Utnapishtim's sacrifice, however, draws the hungry gods "like flies" because they have "forgotten" that they are dependent on the humans for their food. This parody of the gods' behavior is inconceivable in the biblical narrative. Yahweh is never portrayed as forgetful, unjust, or dependent on humankind for nourishment. Instead, there is an almost mechanical consistency to God's actions during the flood, including a "wake-up call" when "God remembered Noah" (8:1) and brought the catastrophe to an end.

Having a God who is so "in control" provides the reassurance needed for the surviving remnant to start again. The story, therefore, demonstrates, as so many of the biblical narratives do, who is the true God. There is no question who has been in charge the entire time. There is no sense of nature out of control and left to expend its destructive energies as in the Gilgamesh Epic. Instead, the majesty of command orchestrates every facet of the story, ensuring the respect due Yahweh.

The Wilderness Experience

Symbolically, the wilderness represents that region of chaos where no person or people have an identity. It is a place of abandonment and struggle, where the only hope for survival is through the intervention of God. The wilderness provides one more means of answering the questions, Who is truly God? and, What is the covenant relationship that binds us to this deity? The Israelites will discover that the God who fulfills the covenant, providing "land and children," is the same God who can safely lead the people through places of chaos and disorder into a promised land. This place of safety will be one where chaos never reigns except when the people themselves transform it into a wilderness.

The Cycle of Wilderness Experience

Because the Israelites viewed all time and all events as cyclical, it is to be expected that there will be one wilderness experience after another throughout their history. The basic assumption is that humans will repeatedly fail in their attempts to stave off disaster and yet another entrance into the wilderness. They will therefore be forced to purify themselves through the pain, dislocation, and loss that is the nature of the wilderness. However, once this process is completed, a remnant will emerge ready once again to resume the relationship with God.

Technically, the first expression of the wilderness experience can be found in the story of the expulsion from Eden. Adam and Eve lived an idyllic existence in the garden of Eden—a place without work, pain, or sorrow, and a place closest to God's presence. As is the case with every example of the wilderness experience, the humans rebel, breaking the rules that have been set down for them, and as a result are forced from a world of perfect order into the unordered chaos of the outside world. There they will be forced to reshape their lives to ultimately find their way back to God.

Abraham also finds himself and his household in a type of wilderness as they attempt to claim and then pass on the right to the promised land. The journey from Mesopotamia to Canaan to Egypt and back to Canaan involves a series of tests of faith and a learning curve as the ancestors learn to trust in the covenant promise. Still, they ultimately abandon the land for a time in favor of a "better life" in Egypt, and this leads them into the first fully developed wilderness experience.

The exodus event, which includes the wilderness experience, provides the model for all subsequent expressions of this theme. The Israelites leave a place of bondage, but also a place of established order. When they are led by Moses into the desert, they begin a journey toward identity and self-realization, but they must first traverse the wilderness to reach their goal.

From the Red Sea through the Wilderness

The story of the crossing of the Red Sea is really the entrance into the wilderness for the Israelites. Before reaching the crisis point, they physically and spiritually have to face a major transition in their lives. Yahweh leads them in the form of a pillar of cloud during the day and a pillar of fire at night. They travel by a "roundabout" route southward into "the wilderness toward the Red Sea" (Ex. 13:18) and then are instructed to make camp. Realizing that they are totally dependent on Moses' and Yahweh's direction, the people show their first sign of wavering when they see the Egyptian army pursuing them. Their "murmuring," or complaining, sets a tone of "What have you done for me lately?" that characterizes the consistent inability of these people to cope with present danger or hardship (14:11–12).

At this point, they must pass through chaos, just as Gilgamesh crosses the "Sea of Death" to reach the Eden-like land of Dilmun in the Mesopotamian heroic epic. Yahweh displays **transcendent** power in parting the waters (another image of chaos in ancient Near Eastern thought found in Marduk's slaying of Tiamat in the *Enuma Elish* creation epic) and in providing them with safe passage to a new region. The celebration of victory over the Egyptians and the god-king, the pharaoh, is given voice in the "Song of the Sea" (Ex. 15:1–18):

> I will sing to the LORD, for he has triumphed gloriously; horse and rider he has thrown into the sea. (Ex. 15:1)

However, the enthusiasm and public acknowledgment of Yahweh's power are short-lived. The people must still traverse the Sinai wilderness to reach the mountain of God and be formally renewed in their covenant relationship with Yahweh. That is the next test of their ability to cope with the wilderness and the uncertainties of life in obeying a God that they are only getting to know again.

Sinai Trek

Almost immediately the high spirits of the people are dashed in the face of the hardships they must face in the Sinai Peninsula. This very harsh landscape has little water or vegetation and is difficult to cross because of the very hot temperatures and the lofty mountains that bar passage in many places. It is in this place of desolation that the real meaning of wilderness is made plain to the Israelites. It is therefore appropriate that this is also the place in the narrative where doubt, in the form of the murmuring motif comes into full play again:

Murmuring Motif

- Faced with famine, thirst, or some other nagging concern, the Israelites begin to murmur against Moses' leadership and against a God who allows this to happen to them
- Angered at such an ungrateful people, Yahweh punishes them in a **culling process** designed to eliminate the unfaithful
- Moses prays for the people, asking God to relent (compare the Atrahasis Epic)

- Because of Moses' prayer and the repentance of the people, God removes the plague and provides food, water, and protection from enemies

This cycle of murmuring, punishment, repentance, and provision is characteristic of the Israelites' reaction to the wilderness experience. The primary purpose here is a discernment process. If the people are to achieve full realization of their identity as the "chosen of God," they must understand which God they are serving. They must be instructed repeatedly on the question, Who is the true God?

The answer to that question in the wilderness comes in two forms. The first is in the form of the needed provisions. So, for example, in Exodus 15:22–25, the people cry out for drinkable water in place of the brackish, bitter water they find at the oasis of Marah. Moses, the intercessor, prays to God on their behalf, and God responds by giving Moses the knowledge to sweeten the waters (compare the miracle by Elisha in 2 Kings 2:21–22). The second part of the answer to the question of who is the God we will worship comes in the form of a very pointed injunction. The people are reminded of their obligation to listen to God's voice, heed and obey the divine commandments, and do what is right in the light of these statutes (compare with the creedal statement in Ex. 19:4–6). If they do this, they will be able to avoid the plagues imposed on their enemies and benefit from being the people of "the LORD who heals you" (Ex. 15:26).

As is so often the case in the biblical narratives, the Israelites keep falling into the trap of unbelief or ingratitude for what God has previously provided. Because they have been warned of the consequences of this unfaithful and disobedient behavior, the justice of God's imposing the culling process on them is quite logical. The fact that it happens so often, like the ten plagues in Egypt, suggests that it was intended to serve a didactic purpose for later generations of Israelites. One would think that one or two harsh lessons would be sufficient to get the point across, but teaching theory has always relied on repetition. The only ameliorating factor in these stories is Moses' intercession, which first prevents God from killing all the Israelites in a single stroke (Num. 14:13–19) and then stops the plague (Num. 16:41–50).

Culling Process

- Three thousand Israelites are executed by Levites at Moses' command for worshiping the golden calf (Ex. 32:25–29)
- The people complain about their misfortunes, and the fire of the Lord burns some outlying parts of the camp at Taberah ("burning") in Num. 11:1–3
- The "rabble" who craved meat instead of a steady diet of manna are struck with a plague at Kibroth-hattaavah ("Graves of craving") in Num. 11:33–34
- The spies who brought an unfavorable report of Canaan and then raised an uproar against Moses' leadership die in a plague (Num. 14:36–38)
- The Levites—Korah, Dathan, and Abiram—revolt against Moses' leadership, and they and their households are swallowed up in an earthquake (Num. 16:1–35); a plague kills 14,700 who subsequently rebelled (Num. 16:41–50)
- Complaints about the food and lack of water result in a plague of poisonous snakes, ended only when Moses sets up a bronze serpent in the camp (Num. 21:4–9)

Some comparison could be made between this culling process and the instructions given to the Mesopotamian hero Atrahasis. In the epic story, the gods were upset with the growing human population and determined to use a variety of means to reduce the numbers significantly. Among the methods were drought and famine, plagues, and finally a great flood. Each attempt is foiled, however, when Atrahasis is told by the god Ea to single out the god specifically responsible for the calamity and worship that god alone. This put such a strain on the other gods who also were dependent on human sacrifices for their sustenance that they relented each time.

The planned reduction in the human population in the Mesopotamian epic, however, was simply meant to relieve the gods of a noisy creation. In the wilderness experience of the Israelites, the unfaithful were culled from the tribes so that they could no longer contaminate the rest of the people. Eventually, all the Israelites who had left Egypt as adults, except Joshua and Caleb, die in the wilderness (Num. 14:20–24; 28–35), and a new, more faithful generation embarks on the conquest of the land.

Prophetic Examples of the Remnant Theme

By far the greatest number of examples of the remnant theme is in the prophetic materials. This is understandable, since by the eighth century B.C.E. historical events were overtaking the nations of Israel and Judah. The Assyrian empire was expanding in the period after 800 B.C.E., and as this seemingly unstoppable force moved closer to Palestine and began to tighten its grip over the economic and political affairs of the entire region, the people were once again faced with the need to make a decision. Were they to accept the Assyrian gods as more powerful than Yahweh, or were they to see, with the prophet Isaiah, that Assyria was "the rod" of God's anger (Isa. 10:5), sent to punish the unfaithful Israelites? Over the next two centuries, the people of Israel and Judah made their decision. In both kingdoms a segment of the people accommodated themselves to the "dominant" culture (Assyrian, Babylonian, and Persian) and were assimilated into their indistinguishable masses. For those who chose to remain loyal to Yahweh, the prophets served as a lightning rod, continually reminding them of their obligations to Yahweh and warning them of the consequences of disobedience to the law.

What follows is a chronological survey of the use of the remnant theme by the Hebrew prophets. Some prophets are quite elaborate, whereas others simply lay the issue out in the barest possible terms. This may be based on the personality and educational level of the individual prophet, or it may simply be consistent with the overall tone of the prophet's message. In any case, it should be noted that no prophetic voice would be necessary if the people were in compliance with the covenant. Thus, the primary purpose of the prophet is to point out the people's failure. This comes in the form of an indictment, in chilling detail, of covenantal violations. The prophets then provide the warning that a just God chooses to issue to ensure that the righteous among the covenantal community have the opportunity to survive the coming divine punishment.

Amos and Hosea

Amos is described in the text as a herdsman and tree dresser (Am. 7:14) from the village of Tekoa in the Judean hill country. His manner of speech is quite brusque, and he shows very little patience with the people of the Northern Kingdom of Israel. This may be simply because he is from the Southern Kingdom and thus feels no political ties to Israel, but it also displays the down-to-earth and practical mind of a small farmer. Standing within the precincts of the royal shrine at Bethel, he characterizes the wealthy and powerful in Israel as those "who trample the head of the poor into the dust of the earth" (2:7). He has no desire to make allowances for greedy merchants who complain about lost business during religious holidays (8:5a) or for landowners who sell the needy into debt slavery for the price of a pair of sandals (2:6b). Amos also condemns their insincere worship practices, stating that God finds their sacrifices unacceptable and their sacred music to be only noise without meaning (5:21–24). As a champion of the covenant, Amos sees much that is out of joint in the Israel of the first half of the eighth century B.C.E.

In the process of delivering his very harsh message, Amos leaves little hope for the nation of Israel. Perhaps this is why there is only a very brief use of the remnant theme in chapter 5. Here, without much elaboration, he tells the people to seek God and live (5:4, 6) so that Yahweh will have justification to relent and lessen their punishment (compare the much longer expression of this idea in Jer. 7:3–15). However, almost in the same breath, the prophet warns Israel against having any confidence in its shrines or the monarchy. With the memory of the division of the kingdom at the end of the ninth century and **Jeroboam's sin** (1 Kings 12:25–33) as background to his message, Amos does not seem to really believe that there is even a glimmer of hope that Israel and its people will repent and therefore survive the coming destruction. He even refers to the "remnant of Joseph"

(= Israel) before the nation has been culled by foreign invaders (Am. 5:15). In light of such a gloomy future, Amos does not waste words on deaf ears. He simply tells the people all that they need to know to live and leaves it to them to act on this advice. Because Israel was enjoying a period of peace and prosperity at that time (the result of Assyria's conquest of Israel's chief rival, Syria, in 802 B.C.E.), some Israelites were envisioning a glorious day of restoration. Amos warns them not to build up false hopes by anticipating a triumphant "day of the LORD" (Am. 5:18–20), for it will bring them judgment, not greater prosperity. This very earthy prophet, drawing on his life experiences, prefers to use the pastoral images of his country background. He describes the unrepentant people of Israel as "summer fruit" (8:2)—sweet and full of initial promise, but quick to decay and to become worthless. Such a powerful image surely must have struck a note with some of the Israelites in the face of growing Assyrian power. But on the horizon, King Tiglath-pileser III (744–727 B.C.E.) moved inexorably westward into Syro-Palestine, absorbing the smaller states and transforming them into his reluctant vassals.

Hosea witnessed this same period, although it is believed that his message was delivered somewhat later than Amos' and therefore closer to the time of Israel's ultimate destruction. Because Hosea was from Israel and was therefore speaking to his own people, his message shows greater empathy as well as a real urgency that the people hear and to which they respond. Thus, he uses his own dysfunctional marriage with Gomer as the basis of an enacted prophecy designed to demonstrate to the people the consequences of their unfaithfulness to Yahweh.

The marriage metaphor in Hosea parallels the role of the prophet with the role of God in relationship with Israel. Hosea's concerns as Gomer's husband matches God's as Israel's covenantal partner. The infidelity of Hosea's wife can thus be equated with Israel's idolatry. When it becomes evident to Hosea that Gomer has taken other men into her bed, he first tries to reason with her by having their children speak with her in the hope that she will abandon her lovers (Hos. 2:2). In this instance, the "children" in the metaphor may also represent the people of Israel reasoning with themselves or their leaders after the prophet has confronted them with the truth of their precarious position. However, when reason fails, Hosea severely punishes Gomer. He first secludes her ("hedge up her way with thorns and…a wall," 2:6), strips her of the jewelry that is associated with the worship of other gods (2:3), and eventually drives her from his home and divorces her (2:9–12). This final act is symbolized by his withdrawing grain, wine, and other products that were her due as a wife in good standing (see the "marital rights" require- ments in Ex. 21:10). Metaphorically, then, the withholding of the products of the land, the reversal of fertility, is a sign of God's displeasure (see Isa. 5:5–6) and signals an end of the covenant agreement, just as it signals the end of Hosea's mar- riage. This breakdown of the covenantal arrangement had also been signaled by the name of Hosea's third child, *Lo-ammi,* "Not My People." Such a complete rejection drives the people into the chaos of the wilderness of exile just as Gomer is driven from Hosea's house.

Exile and destruction, however, cannot be the end of the story. Ultimately, Yahweh seeks to restore the nation, once it is made clear that unfaithful Israel is willing, post-punishment, to obey the covenant agreement. As the metaphor continues, Hosea agrees to take Gomer back if she agrees to renounce her other lovers/Baals forever and freely acknowledges him/Yahweh solely as her lord (Hos. 2:14–20). Gomer's return is matched by Hosea's acknowledgment of their children as his heirs (see the Code of Hammurabi ##170–71 for the father's granting of heir status with the formula statement "My children"). Their rights had been questioned since they had been declared the "children of whore- dom" (Hos. 2:4). Now that they have been given full inheritance rights, the future of the covenant is secure. This metaphor thus takes on a similar character to the search for the heir motif in the ancestral narratives (see the chapter on covenant). The mean- ings of the children's symbolic names also are turned around as fertility is returned to the land and a new covenantal relation- ship is put in place (2:21–23).

One additional way in which the prophet describes this pro- cess of reconciliation with a righteous remnant of Israel is his allusion to the Valley of Achor (Hos. 2:15). This was the place where one of Joshua's soldiers, Achan, and his family had been stoned to death for Achan's violation of the herem. The city of Jericho, its inhabitants, and all its goods, had been "dedicated" to God as a sacrifice. By stealing from the loot captured at Jericho, Achan had defiled the Israelites as a whole (Josh. 7:22–26). The execution of Achan along with his family was based on the legal principle of **corporate responsibility,** which makes an entire household a single legal entity and thus subject to reward or punishment as a whole. This act expiated the nation's sin, and the conquest of Canaan could then continue without further interruption. Hosea thus makes the allusion to Achor to demonstrate that Gomer's sin, while terrible, was not necessarily fatal to the marriage or the nation. God/Hosea could restore the relationship if Gomer/Israel truly resumed her faithfulness to Hosea/Yahweh. Gomer thus represents a purified, restored remnant of the nation worthy to resume a relationship with God.

Isaiah of Jerusalem

The book of Isaiah represents at least two time periods. Isaiah of Jerusalem (chaps. 1–39) is a contemporary of the prophets Hosea and Micah and functions between 742–687 B.C.E. There is also a postexilic voice of Isaiah, probably that of a school of Isaiah thought that had survived the exile period, found in chapters 40–66. Each segment of the book shares certain themes and distinct vocabulary, and, thus, examples are drawn from both periodically, although their distance in time are noted to keep them separate. Because of his elaborate **call narrative** (Isa. 6) and his emphasis on the temple and the Davidic monarchy, it is believed that Isaiah of Jerusalem was a member of the priestly community and high-ranking enough to obtain an audience with the king. During his prophetic ministry, Isaiah witnessed the destruction of the Northern Kingdom of Israel by the Assyrian king Sargon II in 722 B.C.E. and the invasion and devastation of Judah in 701 and 688 B.C.E. by King Sennacherib (Isa. 36–37). His dealings with Judah's kings, Ahaz and Hezekiah, brought mixed results. This further demonstrates the problems the monarchy has in dealing with the political realities of its time while the prophets encourage the kings to hold fast to the

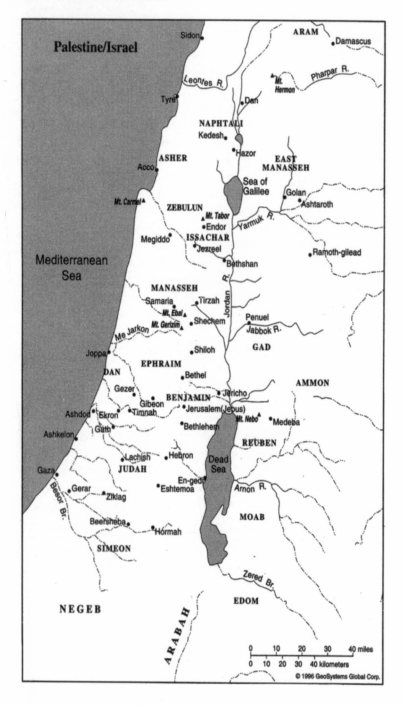

Palestine/Israel

covenant and their faith in Yahweh as divine warrior (see especially Isaiah 7).

Prior to 722 B.C.E., Isaiah's prediction of the punishment of the people of Israel contains a harsh fate for the Northern Kingdom. Their periodic revolts against Assyrian hegemony, as well as the recently aborted Syro-Ephraimitic conflict (730s) in which Israel and Syria had invaded Judah in an attempt to force them into a coalition against Assyria, had ensured the nation's destruction (2 Kings 15:29–16:20). Now, to provide a direct link (a theodicy) between Israel's failures and God's anger, the prophet employs a form of rhetorical reversal. He uses the language of the covenant pledge in Genesis 22:17 in which God promises Abraham that his descendants will be "as numerous as the stars of heaven and as the sand that is on the seashore." Isaiah then indicates that because of their disobedience to God's word only a tiny remnant of that nation's population will survive to return to their land:

Isaiah of Jerusalem (ca. 725 B.C.E.)

For though your people Israel were like the sand of the sea, only a remnant of them will return. Destruction is decreed, overflowing with righteousness. For the Lord GOD of hosts will make a full end, as decreed, in all the earth. (Isa. 10:22–23)

Isaiah of the Exile (ca. 540 B.C.E.)

O that you had paid attention to my commandments! Then your prosperity would have been like a river, and…your offspring would have been like the sand. (Isa. 48:18–19)

It may be that Isaiah speaks his **oracle** during the final days of Israel and recognizes that there is no hope of forestalling the Assyrian tide. His theodicy of punishment can only accept Assyria as "the rod" of God's anger (Isa. 10:5), but there is also a certainty of revenge in which God promises to "punish the arrogant boasting of the king of Assyria" (10:12) and direct divine "anger…to their destruction" (10:25).

Judah will also experience Assyrian occupation, and some cities, like Lachish, will be burned and their populations slaughtered or taken as slaves into exile. But, unlike Israel, their punishment is not to be as extreme, and the capital city of Jerusalem will not fall to the Assyrians. In fact, Isaiah predicts a restoration of the land's fortunes within just three years of the siege of Jerusalem (Isa. 37:30–32). Isaiah seems content that Yahweh's city and temple are left intact despite the claims made by the Assyrians that they had come at the Israelite God's insistence to restore proper worship and depose their rebellious king Hezekiah (36:4–20).

This celebration of Jerusalem's survival was little comfort to the people of Judah's small villages and towns, which had suffered economic ruin and the murder and rape of their people. The contemporary prophet Micah indicts both Samaria and Jerusalem and their leaders for bringing down God's and Assyria's wrath on them (Mic. 1:2–9; 3:10–12). He predicts that because of wicked rulers and corrupt prophets the people will be forced from **Zion**/Jerusalem, and only the survivors will be gathered by God and brought back to the land "like a flock in its pasture" (2:12–13; 4:6–8). This rural prophetic voice sees the purification of God's punishment leading to a new world in which the sources of corruption and the weapons of war are put aside so that God once again reigns over a people who are obedient to the covenant (5:10–15).

In contrast, Isaiah couples his images of the restoration of the remnant and the nation with the assurance that a representative of the Davidic ruling house will lead them. Thus, in Isaiah 11:1–2, he uses the image of a stump—a symbol of the nation cut off by the Assyrian invaders and apparently dead. However, the stump of the nation will display new life: "A shoot shall come out from the stump of Jesse" (David's father). This ruler will have Yahweh's wise counsel and will be the model for a people who must have the knowledge and fear of Yahweh to survive. Similarly, the familiar prediction of the child "born for us" in Isaiah 9:6–7 refers to an idealized Davidic king who, unlike the idolatrous and unfaithful Ahaz (see 2 Kings 16:1–4), can lead the people while still adhering to the covenant.

Jeremiah

The nation of Judah was able to survive for more than a century after the fall of Israel. However, its fate was also tied to the superpower politics of the ancient Near East. When the Assyrian empire disintegrated after the death of Ashurbanipal in 627 B.C.E., the Neo-Babylonian, or Chaldean, empire emerged to take its place. King Nebuchadnezzar briefly brought Babylonian hegemony over Syro-Palestine and in the process destroyed Jerusalem and its temple, bringing the Davidic monarchy to an end. Even the short-lived cultural and political renaissance of Judah's king, Josiah, could not withstand the pressures of outside forces. When Josiah was killed at the Battle of Megiddo in 609 B.C.E., it was clear that Judah was on the brink of a new wilderness experience, and the prophet Jeremiah tried very hard to get this across to the people.

One excellent example of the use of remnant as a predicted condition is in Jeremiah 6:9. The prophet uses the visual image of a vineyard that has already been harvested. Now, however, an angry God "gleans" what remains of this remnant, stripping the branches of all its fruit. What is particularly interesting about this picture is its express relationship to the law in Deuteronomy 24:19–22. As part of their covenantal agreement with Yahweh, the Israelites were required to leave a portion of the harvest for "the alien, the orphan, and the widow." These protected classes were a metaphor for Israel itself. God provided for the nation, one of the weakest on earth, and the nation in turn was expected to care for the weak within its community. Jeremiah's message, which apparently fell on deaf ears according to 6:10, shows God's determination to gather all the people into exile's "basket," just as a hungry widow stretches to break off every bunch of grapes.

Another way in which Jeremiah warns the nation occurs in Jeremiah 18. In this chapter, Jeremiah employs an enacted prophecy, using a scene in the potters' district of the city to provide both the backdrop and the message of his prophecy. While the prophet watched this everyday activity, he saw that the craftsman was dissatisfied with his creation. It may have been misshapen, or perhaps its walls were too thin to withstand firing. Whatever the case, the potter stopped his wheel, reworked the clay into a shapeless lump, and once again began working it to create the desired vessel (Jer. 18:3–4). The explanation of this scene that Jeremiah receives from God is that the clay is the nation of Judah, and Yahweh is the potter. Like the pot being formed on the wheel, the nation had not taken the proper shape according to the desires of its maker (compare with Isa. 29:16). As a result, Yahweh will remold the clay and begin again, using the substance of the clay to shape a new vessel.

This is an excellent example of the remnant theme. There is no mystery here. The prophet can effectively warn the people of inevitable punishment for their failure to obey the stipulations of the covenant. The frustration felt by the craftsman is evident, and it is therefore easy to make the analogy with the divine potter, forced to reassess his creation. What makes this a remnant image is the clay. It is not discarded. Instead, it is saved so that it may be used to create a new pot. In the same way a remnant of the people will be spared in order to restore the nation.

Like Isaiah, Jeremiah also makes an effort to reassure the people that the punishment that they must face at the hands of Babylon is not the end of the nation's hopes. Just as Assyria was dismembered and forgotten, the prophet predicts that God will punish "the king of Babylon and his land" and "restore Israel to its pasture" (Jer. 50:17–19). Then the remnant will be pardoned because the sins of Israel and Judah will be cleansed and seen no more (50:20).

In that new, purified condition, with God's covenant written "on their hearts" (Jer. 31:33), they may once again function as a nation within their own land. This makes Jeremiah's insistence on redeeming a field during the siege of Jerusalem that much more powerful (32:6–15). He is given the option to purchase the land because he is the nearest male relative, and as a rule no household would wish to have a piece of land pass out of the inheritance (see Lev. 25:25–28). There is no practical reason to make the purchase, since there is no possibility that Jeremiah will be able to use the land or make it productive at this point, the end of Judah's political existence. However, the implicit meaning in his writing up the deed and having it witnessed (compare with Abraham in Gen. 23:16–18) is a reiteration of the covenant that promised land and children to Israel. This generation may not enjoy the benefits of the land, for they must once again survive the wilderness, but the land and the promise will be waiting there for their descendants' return.

Ezekiel

Although a contemporary of Jeremiah, the prophet Ezekiel is already in exile by the time he begins to speak. He is in the wilderness and yet must prophesy the destruction of Jerusalem and the gathering of a new host of his people to share his fate in Mesopotamia. Like Isaiah, Ezekiel is a priest and is concerned with issues of **ritual purity**, **liturgy**, and law. Many of the enacted prophecies that he uses center on shocking his audience. For instance, a complete role reversal occurs when this scrupulously clean, priestly figure plays in the dirt with an engraved brick and stick figures to enact the siege of Jerusalem (Ezek. 4:1–3). In another case, he portrays himself as a penitent, lying on his side every day for months (4:4–6). His meager rations stand in sharp contrast to the meals he must have enjoyed as a member of the priestly community (4:9–11, 16–17). Now, however, his evident poverty serves as a symbol of what the nation must suffer in order to purify itself and thereby regain its place as God's chosen people.

A third graphically portrayed prophecy appears in chapter 5. Here the prophet, in what could be described as an example of street theater, is told to shave his head and beard. These are normally acts of persons in mourning, or they serve as signs of those who have been humiliated (see 2 Sam. 10:4). His hair is divided into three piles. The prophet then chops up one pile with a sword, scatters another in the wind, and throws the third pile into the fire. This obviously symbolizes the majority of the people during the fall of Jerusalem. Only a scant few of his hairs, a remnant, are left, and these are bound up in the edges of the prophet's robes (Ezek. 5:3). This is such a visually oriented set of actions that it would be most impressive in the open air where the wind could play its part and the fire and sword could be used effectively. Although it provides no hope for Jerusalem's immediate future, the fact that a remnant is foretold to survive is another expression of hope for the people's survival and restoration.

The opportunity for the survival of a remnant of the people of Judah also appears in Ezekiel 9. This vision is probably a reflection of Ezekiel's understanding of his own exile. There must be an explanation or theodicy to justify why he has been taken away while so many others were allowed to remain in Jerusalem. Now, in this vision of seven men (six executioners and a scribe) he can demonstrate that to be exiled is a sign of membership in the righteous remnant. It also offers hope to those who are still in Jerusalem that some of them will also join this select group.

Ezekiel's oracle either draws upon or is parallel to the passover story (Ex. 12). In that seminal event that marks the origin of the nation as God's people, the Israelites are instructed to mark their doorposts with the blood of the sacrificial lamb (a symbol for the expiation of sins, Ex. 12:6–13). By obeying God's command, they save their lives and are allowed to join in the exodus from Egypt. In Ezekiel's vision, the linen-clad scribe is instructed to place the Hebrew letter *taph* (an x-shape) on the forehead of all those persons who "sigh and groan" over the sins of the nation (Ezek. 9:4). These rituals of mourning (see Ps. 38:8–9) thus identify the righteous so that they may be set aside for survival.

The prophetic oracle also contains elements of the story in Exodus 32 in which Moses orders the Levites to slaughter the people who have worshiped the golden calf. For instance, in both Exodus 32:27 and in Ezekiel 9:5–6, the executioners "pass through" the camp/city to carry out their orders. The righteous are known by their deeds in both stories, and, therefore, it is possible to clearly distinguish those who are to be slain. The executioners in Ezekiel slay without mercy everyone who does not have the mark of innocence, just as the Levites "cull" the camp of the idolaters.

Assurance is also given by God that those who are taken away into exile will be given "sanctuary" by Yahweh in these distant countries. They have not been cut off from the land forever and will eventually be assembled by God and returned to Israel (Ezek. 11:16–17). When they return, all the abominations of idolatry and lawlessness will be swept away because the wilderness experience that the people have endured will transform them. They will have a "new heart" and a "new spirit" placed within them by God and will therefore obey the statutes and ordinances that define the covenant agreement (11:19–20).

Postexilic Wilderness Experience

The reiteration of the wilderness experience in the exilic and postexilic periods plays on the original elements of the wilderness experience in Exodus and Numbers. Like those Israelites, who suffered for forty years in the inhospitable terrain of the Sinai, the exiles suffered a period of social chaos in the midst of an inhospitable nation. The Babylonian conquest of Judah in 598 B.C.E. had given them a taste of what was to come, but in 587, when Jerusalem was captured by Nebuchadnezzar for the second time and the entire city was destroyed, including Solomon's temple, they were inconsolable in their misery (see Ps. 137). Only the reassurances of the prophets Jeremiah (29:10–14) and Ezekiel (34:17–31) offered hope of eventual return and restoration for the descendants of the exiles.

It was sixty years before the exiles from Judah were given the opportunity to return to their homeland. The decrees of the Persian king Cyrus in 538 B.C.E. offered financial assistance for the rebuilding of temples and for provisioning expeditions back to the exiles' homes. As noted in the chapter on "covenant," not all the Israelites took up Isaiah of the Exile's enthusiastic call to return to Zion (Isa. 40:1–5; 43:1–7). Most chose to continue their lives in the lands where they had lived for several generations. Those who did journey back to Palestine found an immense task of rebuilding ahead of them. This may, at least in part, explain why the returned exiles saw themselves as the righteous remnant who now had the right to reclaim the land from those who had remained in Israel. Thus, when the rebuilding of the Jerusalem temple was begun, the returnees ignored or repulsed offers of help from the people who had remained in the land during the exile (see Ezra 4:1–3).

Signs of this self-styled identity of the remnant can be found in the way the postexilic prophets describe the people. For instance, Haggai, a prophet associated with the first group of returnees to Jerusalem (ca. 520 B.C.E.), pointedly refers to his fellows as "the remnant of the people" (Hag. 1:12, 14). This part of his rhetoric refers collectively to Judah's returned leaders and the faithful whom he hopes to inspire to rebuild God's temple. It is possible that a similar postexilic usage is to be found in

2 Chronicles 34:9 in the retelling of Josiah's seventh-century reform (see the original version in 2 Kings 22). In describing the contributions that were brought to help rebuild and cleanse the temple from its idolatrous contamination, the writer uses the phrase "all the remnant of Israel." Since Chronicles is a post-500 B.C.E. version of Israel's history, its use of this expression so similar to Haggai's phrase in the context of similar activities suggests a common understanding of the Jerusalem community in the postexilic period.

The identification of the remnant with a restored Jerusalem community had been a part of Isaiah of Jerusalem's message. In Isaiah 10:20, the prophet refers to a people who no longer have to "lean on the one who struck them, but will lean on the LORD." He points to a day when God "will extend his hand...to recover the remnant that is left of his people" (11:11), and then the "surviving remnant of the house of Judah shall again take root downward, and bear fruit upward" (37:31). Such a prominent theme was easily revived in the postexilic writings of Zechariah. In his visions of the restoration of Zion, he sees the streets of the city "full of boys and girls playing in its streets" (Zech. 8:5). This stands in stark contrast to Jeremiah's horrific sight of the bodies of the slain clogging the streets like cordwood at the time of the city's destruction (Jer. 9:21–22). In this newly cleansed Jerusalem (compare with Isa. 65:17–25), God will "deal with the remnant of this people as in the former days" (Zech. 8:11). All that had been lost will be restored, and the covenant promise of land and children, here identified with the well-watered produce of the ground and the vine, will once again become the possession of "the remnant of this people" (8:12).

CHAPTER 3

Universalism

One of the primary aims of the biblical story is to teach. Its authors recognized that other nations worshiped many gods and that these nations were often successful. Whether the perception was correct or not, it seemed that in most years these nations' crops were plentiful and they were often victorious in battle because of the power of their gods. In the face of these apparently attractive gods, the biblical writers attempted to instruct the Israelites on the nature of their God. They portrayed Yahweh as a caring parent (Hos. 11:1–4), an impartial judge (Ps. 96:10), and a divine warrior (Ex. 15:3)—all images that were also used by the other peoples of the ancient Near East for their gods. Although they were not above telling a good story, the compilers of the biblical materials considered it their most important task to inform the Israelite people: (1) Who really is God? and (2) What powers are at Yahweh's command?

One effective method that the storytellers used was the universalism theme. It is woven throughout the biblical text, although it does change its character during the latter stages of Israelite history in the postexilic period. Initially, the universalism theme is built on a foundation of divine acts of power. It must be proven that Yahweh alone is responsible for the creation of the universe and the maintenance of the natural order. In this way, the **etiological** stories of creation, flood, cosmic battle, and the granting of law and divine direction to humans is **demythologized,** and Yahweh stands supreme. Second, Yahweh must choose a people for whom he will stand as divine patron, divine warrior, and source of all the necessities of life. This is accomplished through the establishment of the covenant with Abraham and the expansion of the covenantal agreement in the giving of the laws to Moses. Further expressions of this second task can be found in establishment of an "everlasting covenant" with the royal house of David, and ultimately the restoration of the exiles from Babylonian captivity. Each of these developments has been discussed in detail in the chapters on covenant and remnant and will not be repeated here.

Elements of the Universalism Theme

- Yahweh performs a feat or set of feats on which to base a reputation of power as "creator God" and divine patron of the Israelite people
- A non-Israelite is attracted to Yahweh and the Israelites by this reputation
- A statement of absolute confidence and faith in Yahweh is made by the non-Israelite
- The concept of monotheism is advanced until it becomes the norm for the Jews in the postexilic period

Once the premise has been proven that Yahweh is all-powerful God and that Israel is under the protection of an invincible divine warrior, the biblical writers can begin to use non-Israelites to demonstrate Yahweh's recognizable force and majesty. The idea behind this strategy is that if these people, who are not a part of the covenant community, can recognize God's supremacy in the universe, that should convince the Israelites that they should obey the covenant and worship only Yahweh. The unashamed statement of faith made by a non-Israelite who is startled and amazed at Yahweh's mastery of all creation serves as a model for the Israelite creedal statement, the **Shema**, in Deuteronomy 6:4: "Hear, O Israel: The LORD is our God, the LORD alone."

In the period after the exile, Yahweh's act of returning the exiles to Palestine becomes the means to convince all nations that there is no other God. This is not to say that they will all be converted to Judaism. Rather, the people of the covenant gain ultimate satisfaction and confidence from the fact that their devotion to Yahweh as the one, true God has been justified to the world. The case has been made at last, and the message in the prophets and in post-500 B.C.E. wisdom literature is now one of universal dominion. It takes Israel much of its history to develop a truly monotheistic religion. The introduction of the universalism theme into the narrative is one of the steps taken by the biblical writers to advance the belief that Yahweh is the one, true God.

Universalism in the Command of Nature

The creation stories of ancient Mesopotamia and Egypt are designed both to explain the origins of the universe and to advance the political fortunes of particular **city-states**. So, for example, the *Enuma Elish* creation epic provides an outline of the early generations of the gods (a **theogony**), which portrays the rise of eighteenth-century B.C.E. Babylon's chief god, Marduk, to the status of chief of the divine assembly. Similarly, the Memphite Theology of Old Kingdom Egypt (2575–2134 B.C.E.) portrays the god Ptah as the supreme creator, while a rival city, Heliopolis, celebrates the god Atum's creative acts. In each of the cases, the supremacy of the creator god is tied to the political prowess of the city for whom the god stands as chief patron. It should be understood, however, that these gods are leaders of a much larger group, or pantheon, of all the gods.

Many similarities exist between ancient Near Eastern creation and flood stories and those found in the biblical narrative. The logical sequence of movement from primordial, watery chaos to an ordered universe is common to each of these stories. However, in the Egyptian and Mesopotamian epics the transition out of chaos is often portrayed as the result of cosmic struggle in which gods are killed or subjugated to the will of other, more powerful deities. For instance, Marduk, the patron god of Babylon, kills Tiamat, the goddess of watery anarchy, and transforms her corpse into the heavens and the earth. In both the Memphite and Heliopolitan creation stories of ancient Egypt, the creator god (Ptah and Ra, respectively) brings the other major gods into being (the Ennead) and then assigns them tasks so that the universe can operate in an ordered manner.

Because the Israelites are said to have come from Mesopotamia originally and to have spent many years in Egypt, it is inconceivable that they would not have been familiar with the religious epics of the major cultures of the Near East. The problem faced by the biblical writers, therefore, was to find a way to use these well-known stories to demonstrate the singular power of Yahweh. However, they had to do this without direct reference to the existence of other gods. The only way in which the gods of other nations might be mentioned would be as the forces of nature that would be created or manipulated by Yahweh. For the Israelite God to be recognized as universal, and unchallenged, the biblical writers had to compose their epics free of cosmic battle. Yahweh's actions must always be those of a self-confident, transcendent being.

Creation and Flood Epics

The method employed by the biblical writers to demythologize the creation and flood stories was, in fact, a nearly silent polemic against all other gods. Instead of denouncing the gods of wood and stone (Isa. 37:19) or ridiculing them as powerless "scarecrows" (Jer. 10:5), the authors of the creation and flood stories ignore the possibility of the existence of powers other than Yahweh. Only Tiamat's name survives, in Genesis 1:2, in the word *tehom*, and then simply as a noun for the "great deep" that existed prior to God's creation.

Whereas Marduk is said to divide Tiamat's body in half to form the heavens and the earth, Yahweh calls the world into being with a word. There is no challenge here, no rivals, and no need to maintain vigilant supremacy over other gods. Only the Egyptian hymn to Ptah approaches the majesty of Yahweh's creation:

> Ptah gave life to every member of the Ennead and to the soul of each. Each came into being through the thoughts in his heart and the words of his tongue...The thoughts of the heart of Ptah and the words of the tongue of Ptah guide all the

thoughts and all the words of humans, and of all
life. (*OTP*, p. 4)

However, this Old Kingdom epic cannot resist falling into polemic against other creator gods and other cities that claim to house the supreme deity of Egypt. Ptah is said to be more powerful because he speaks creation into being, like Yahweh in Genesis 1:3–26, while Atum of Heliopolis creates through a form of masturbation.

There is also a conscious theme running through the biblical creation story designed to place humanity in a position as God's supreme creation. A caring God fashions humans in the divine image, blesses them with the ability to be fertile, and grants them "dominion" over all other creatures (Gen. 1:2–28). The creation of humans in the Mesopotamian epics casts a shadow of subservience over them. In the *Enuma Elish*, humans are formed from the blood of the rebel god Kingu for the sole purpose of performing the tasks that the gods do not wish to perform. When their numbers grow too large and begin to disturb the sleep of the gods, plagues and other calamities are imposed on them as forms of population control. Eventually, a second creation takes place, in the Atrahasis Epic, in which two gods compete to shape beings whose "gifts" are infertility, religious celibacy, and stillborn children. This stands in stark contrast to the nurturing, parentlike attitude of Yahweh toward Adam and Eve. God provides them with a paradise to live in, employment in the garden, and limits on their behavior. When the humans exceed their limits and are forced into the real world of work, pain, and death, God does not abandon them. Instead, their blessing of fertility is reinforced with the birth of children. Their world is not perfect, but it does include a God who is just and capable of providing them with their needs.

The stories of the flood in both the Mesopotamian epics and the Bible follow a basic literary pattern. They all include a hero who is warned by a god, builds a boat, and fills it with animals so that life can begin once again after the flood. Where they differ is in the emphasis in the biblical text on a single, transcendent God, who actually cares about creation. In the Gilgamesh flood epic, the god Ea warns Utnapishtim, but only indirectly (through a reed hut's wall) and not because the hero deserves to be saved—he is just in the right place at the right time. When he constructs his ark, it is for protection from the elements of nature gone wild as well as from the gods. Utnapishtim has no expectations of assistance from any divine being and thus relies on the magical shape (cube) of his ark and its relationship (segmented levels) to the ziggurat temples of Mesopotamia. After he has ridden out the storm, the hero builds an altar and makes a sacrifice, but again this is a means of warding off further problems rather than a thank offering.

In the Genesis account, God evaluates a creation that has become flawed by human wickedness. The Mesopotamian epics either place the blame on the excessive noise caused by the mass of humanity (Atrahasis) or give no explanation other than divine desire for a flood (Gilgamesh). In contrast, the Israelite God takes the responsibility to cleanse the world of its corruption with a flood. As noted in the chapter on remnant, this decision also includes the necessity to provide an opportunity for the righteous among humanity to survive. Thus, Noah and his family are warned, given instructions on the construction of an ark and the composition of its cargo, and then, during the flood, are protected from the destructive elements. In fact, God personally closes the hatches of the ark (Gen. 7:16)—a gesture much like a parent tucking a child into bed and assuring her that the dangers of the night cannot reach her.

A conscious effort is also made by the biblical storytellers to show that Yahweh is in complete control during the flood. They know that their audience is aware of the comic elements in the Gilgamesh epic. In that story the gods must collectively pool their powers in order to generate the energy needed to start the flood. But then they cannot control its force. They cower like dogs, cry out in fear, and demonstrate quite clearly that they have made a mistake. Furthermore, when the floodwaters have receded and Utnapishtim makes his sacrifice, the gods flock to the altar like hungry flies because they have "forgotten" that they need humans to feed them through offerings.

Yahweh, on the other hand, skillfully marshals the forces of the storm without any companions. There is no hint of divine fear during the height of the flood. Instead a brooding presence, similar to that prior to creation, watches the reversal of the creation cycle as all living things are destroyed (Gen. 7:17–24). And, as in the creation story, when Noah makes his offering of thanksgiving for the survival of his family, God certifies it as good (compare Gen. 1:4, 10, 31 with 8:21).

In these familiar stories, the biblical writers take the opportunity to demonstrate the singularity of their God. The universalism theme in these examples makes it clear that Yahweh is the only true God, who is fully in control of the universe as well as the nations of the earth. Therefore, the Israelites are enjoined to recognize this fact, set aside the idols of their neighbors, and adhere to their covenant obligations to worship Yahweh alone.

Contests between the Gods

Although no hint of cosmic battle is found in the primordial stories of Genesis (compare the poetic battles with Leviathan in Ps. 74:14 and 104:26), the reality was that other gods were worshiped in the ancient Near East. In some cases, the nations who worshiped these gods dominated or threatened the Israelites. As a result, Yahweh was forced occasionally to take them on—even if these deities had no reality outside the imagination of their worshipers. There are many examples of these contests, but I will concentrate on only a few to make the point clear.

Exodus Event

Perhaps the most important of the contests between Yahweh and another god is to be found in the story of the exodus (note the parallel account in Gen. 12:10–20). This formative epic depicts the saving act of Yahweh, freeing the Israelites from Egyptian bondage and demonstrating that the god-king pharaoh is no match for a God in full control of creation. The memory of this contest and its result will be echoed throughout the rest of the biblical text:

> I am the LORD your God, who brought you out of the land of Egypt, out of the house of slavery. (Ex. 20:2; **Prologue to Ten Commandments**)

> For ask now about former ages, long before your own, ever since the day that God created human beings on the earth...Has any people ever heard

> the voice of a god speaking out of a fire, as you have heard, and lived? Or has any god ever attempted to go and take a nation for himself from the midst of another nation, by trials, by signs and wonders, by war, by a mighty hand and an outstretched arm, and by terrifying displays of power, as the LORD your God did for you in Egypt before your very eyes? (Deut. 4:32–34)

> Also I brought you up out of the land of Egypt, and led you forty years in the wilderness, to possess the land of the Amorite. (Am. 2:10)

> And now, O Lord our God, who brought your people out of the land of Egypt with a mighty hand and made your name renowned even to this day...(Dan. 9:15)

In fact, the often-quoted statement becomes the basis of God's justification for punishing the Israelites. They had been warned at the time of the exodus to obey the stipulations of the covenant and now must face the consequences of their actions (see Jer. 7:21–26; 32:21–23).

Although the story of the exodus is a serious narrative, ironic as well as comic aspects are embedded in the successive episodes. Moses and Aaron are frustrated by the stubbornness of both the pharaoh and the Israelites. In fact, it almost seems as if the Israelites would prefer that Moses just go away and leave them in slavery (Ex. 5:20–21). The sequence of plagues draws upon the pharaoh's role as guardian and provider for his people. The polluting of the Nile River, the diseases and insects that sicken the animals, and the hail that damages the crops all testify to the failure of the god-king to carry out his duties. But are ten plagues really necessary? What is the point of so much repetition?

Perhaps the answer is to be found once again in the didactic nature of the biblical narrative. In order to systematically assure the Israelites of the power of their God in relation to all other divine claimants, it is necessary to completely strip the pharaoh of all of his divine attributes and then, in the end, to deprive him and the people of Egypt of hope for the future. By taking the "firstborn," Yahweh does more than ecological damage. This "Passover" act marks God's chosen from among all other peoples and destroys a generation of Egyptians who had depended on their gods to protect them.

Having accomplished these things, the Deuteronomic writers can look back from their vantage point at the end of the monarchic period and state that the exodus and Sinai events are the basis upon which to "acknowledge that the LORD is God; there is no other besides him" (Deut. 4:35). Monotheism is made plausible by the time of the postexilic period because the people have come to accept their epic history. The God who brought them out of Egypt, spoke to them out of the fire, and drove other nations out before them is the "God in heaven above and on the earth beneath" (Deut. 4:39).

Contest on Mount Carmel

Although not as spectacular as the exodus event, Elijah's contest with the prophets of Baal on Mount Carmel provides the same sort of proof-text for the universalism theme. Once again the faithful of Israel, much reduced by the systematic elimination of Yahweh's prophets by Jezebel, Ahab's Phoenician wife, are faced with a situation in which it appears that another god is more powerful than Yahweh (1 Kings 18:4). Elijah had set the stage for the contest by predicting a three-year drought for Israel. This was the perfect prelude to the confrontation because Baal was a storm-god, whose life-giving rains were supposed to bring fertility to the land:

> Moreover Baal, will send abundance of his rain, abundance of moisture with snow; he will utter his voice in the clouds, (he will send) his flashing to the earth with lightning. (UT 51, V. 68–69; Gray, p. 402)

If Baal could not produce rain, the people had to conclude either that they had angered the god and were being punished or that Baal did not exist and Yahweh was punishing them for their idolatry.

To resolve this set of conflicting conclusions, Elijah challenges Ahab to send the four hundred fifty prophets of Baal and four hundred prophets of Asherah to Mount Carmel (1 Kings 18:19), where they could publicly call on their god to end the drought. The Israelites assembled around the base of this mountain, which overlooks the Mediterranean coast, to witness the contest of power. The scene conjures up a picture very similar to that of the people camped around Mount Sinai after the trek through the Sinai wilderness. Moses climbed up to speak with God, and the people were able to see and hear manifestations of God's power in the thunder and lightning and thick clouds that enveloped the mountain (Ex. 19:16–18). Now it is a "new Moses" who champions Yahweh and attempts to gain the people's confidence from the heights of Mount Carmel.

Elijah calls on the people to make a firm decision: "If the LORD is God, follow him; but if Baal, then follow him" (1 Kings 18:21). The aspects of the competition on Mount Carmel give the people the opportunity to discern the proper choice. Both sides have an equal chance. They each construct an altar, sacrifice a bull, and call upon their god. It is simply up to the deity to respond with fire and a break in the drought. What adds both tension and a comic overlay to the narrative is the image of the Baal prophets dancing around the altar, cutting themselves, and repeating a litany, "O Baal, answer us!" for hours on end (18:26–29). Although Elijah had been very businesslike in making his proposal to King Ahab, he takes advantage of the prophets' failure to arouse Baal by mocking them and their efforts. He tells them to cry out louder and then, cynically, suggests a variety of reasons for Baal's silence: "He is meditating, or he has wandered away, or he is on a journey, or perhaps he is asleep and must be awakened" (18:27). What Elijah is actually doing is challenging Baal's very existence, sarcastically saying, "Surely he is a god."

Of course, just because a god fails to answer prayer or respond with fire from heaven when asked to do so does not mean that the god does not exist—or at least this is the argument with which the prophets of Baal must content themselves. Elijah has given them their chance and now takes his turn. He uses his staged performance to draw on several images of Israelite tradition. First he rebuilds an altar that once was dedicated to Yahweh on this site. He uses twelve stones to represent the twelve tribes of Israel, just as Joshua did in constructing a monument after miraculously crossing the Jordan River to begin the conquest of the land (Josh. 4:1–7). The trench that is dug around the altar and the threefold drenching of the wood serves the practical purpose of preventing any suggestion that a stray spark ignited the sacrifice. It also reminds the people of their need for rain after a three-year drought (compare with 2 Sam. 24:13).

When Elijah calls on God to respond, it is to demonstrate to the Israelites that Yahweh is in fact the God (1 Kings 18:37). Now it becomes clear why Elijah suggested that the test of a divine response include fire from heaven. This is one of the attributes of Baal, the god of storms. But Baal did not answer the prophets' pleas. It is Yahweh who uses the lightning to consume the sacrifice, the altar, and the water-filled trench. Now, in place of the litany chanted by the Baal prophets, an amazed audience of Israelites chants the recognition formula: "The LORD indeed is God; the LORD indeed is God" (18:39). This concludes the first phase of the contest and is also the signal for the mass execution of the Baal prophets according to the Deuteronomic law to kill those who advocate false worship (Deut. 13:1–5).

To bring a completely successful end to the proceedings, Elijah must show his own faith in Yahweh to end the drought and bring rain. He invites Ahab to relax with a meal, a symbol of covenant or treaty obligation, while the prophet bows in submission. His servant is instructed to ascend the side of Mount Carmel facing the sea and watch for the coming storm clouds. Significantly, this is repeated seven times, the prime number associated with creation, and then relief comes, first with a small cloud and then a warning to Ahab that he must hurry down the mountain before the wadis fill with floodwaters and leave him stranded (1 Kings 18:41–45). In this way, Yahweh, the creator god and fulfiller of the covenant promise of fertility, defeats Baal.

Yahweh has once again won a contest between gods, but Elijah's flight from Jezebel's wrath demonstrates that this is not conclusive in the minds of the Israelites or their leaders. The prophet spends some time in the wilderness before he finds the courage and the determination to return and complete his mission (1 Kings 19). Ultimately, it requires the elimination of the institutions of cult and palace and their own wilderness experience (the exile) for the Israelite people to be able to discern the reality of Yahweh's universal power.

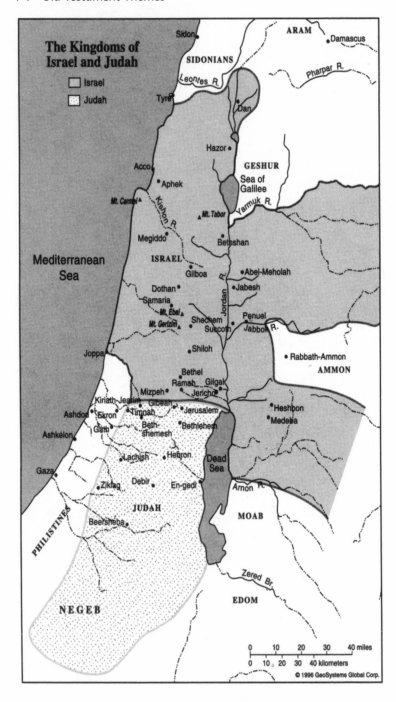

The Kingdoms of
Israel and Judah

☐ Israel
▨ Judah

ARAM
Damascus
Sidon
SIDONIANS
Leontes R.
Pharpar R.
Tyre
Dan
Hazor
GESHUR
Acco
Sea of
Galilee
Aphek
Mt. Carmel
Kishon R.
Mt. Tabor
Yarmuk R.
Megiddo
Bethshan
Mediterranean
Sea
ISRAEL
Gilboa
Abel-Meholah
Jordan R.
Dothan
Jabesh
Samaria
Mt. Ebal
Penuel
Mt. Gerizim
Shechem
Succoth
Jabbok R.
Shiloh
Joppa
Rabbath-Ammon
Bethel
AMMON
Ramah
Gilgal
Mizpeh
Jericho
Kiriath-Jearim
Gibeah
Ashdod
Ekron
Timnah
Jerusalem
Heshbon
Medeba
Ashkelon
Gath
Beth-
shemesh
Bethlehem
Lachish
Hebron
Dead
Sea
Gaza
Ziklag
Debir
En-gedi
Arnon R.
JUDAH
MOAB
PHILISTINES
Beersheba
Zered Br.
EDOM
NEGEB

0   10   20   30   40 miles
0   10   20   30   40 kilometers

© 1996 GeoSystems Global Corp.

Universalism and Non-Israelites

Ultimately, the purpose of the universalism theme is to convince the Israelites that not only is their God a powerful being, but Yahweh is the only God in the entire universe. It is therefore not enough to demonstrate Yahweh's power through feats of strength or the defeat of other gods. There can be no claims of monotheism as long as other gods are given any recognition whatsoever. One of the principal ways in which the biblical writers attempt to showcase Yahweh's singular authority is in a series of narratives in which non-Israelites make statements of faith in God's power.

Balaam and the Transjordanian Trek

As noted in the chapter on remnant, the unfaithfulness of the Israelites once they had escaped Egypt in the exodus led to a severe punishment. The entire generation of adults who had followed Moses into the Sinai desert was condemned to die over a forty-year period of wanderings (Num. 14:20–24). The purification of the chosen people prepared them to accept Joshua's leadership once Moses had died, and to mount the military conquest of the land of Palestine. Part of the preparations for entering the promised land included a series of conflicts with peoples in Transjordan. The Israelites' trek begins with the crossing of the Zered River, the boundary between Edom and Moab. This takes them into the territory of the Amorite tribes ruled by kings Sihon and Og (Num. 21:10–35). With the assistance of Yahweh, the divine warrior (see a similar victory in Ex. 17:8–13 over the Amalekites), the Israelites were successful in defeating these kings and taking control of their lands (principally Gilead and Bashan).

These battles seem to be a prelude to the conflict with Moab described in Numbers 22–24. In this narrative a foreign prophet named Balaam is introduced, and the biblical writers use him to advance the universalism theme. What is particularly interesting about this story is that Balaam is known outside the Bible as a prophet:

> The divine assembly appeared to Balaam, son of
> Beor, at night. He dreamed he heard El pronounce
> a death sentence on his city. He watched as the

> divine assembly announced the beginning of a
> drought that would burn the land of his city like a
> raging fire. When Balaam got up the next morn-
> ing, he began to fast and to lament bitterly. The
> people of the city asked: "Balaam, son of Beor,
> why do you fast? Why do you mourn?" So Balaam
> agreed to tell them his dream. (*OTP*, pp. 124–25)

By using a well-known character, the biblical storytellers drew on the popularity of this prophetic figure to advance Yahweh's authority. Throughout the narrative, Balaam is assumed to have the power to bless and to curse in the name of God, but no god is ever referred to in the story other than Yahweh. This is remarkable, since Balaam is a non-Israelite and presumably is associated with many other gods (as in the Deir 'Alla inscription quoted above). Certainly, when Balak, the king of Moab, hires Balaam, he expects the prophet to draw on the power of all the gods to rain down curses on the enemy. But the king apparently ignores Balaam's repeated disclaimer that he can only speak the words given to him by God/Yahweh (Num. 22:38; 23:12).

It should be no surprise, then, when Balaam fails to carry out his employer's commission. This is despite the fact that the king of Moab had carefully orchestrated what should have been an effective ward of his country from the invading Israelites. He had taken Balaam up onto three of the hills overlooking his territory, constructed seven altars on each one, and sacrificed seven bulls and seven rams on each. It is inconceivable that so much effort would come to nothing. Surely, the gods of the land would channel their power through Balaam and curse his enemies. But the king is disappointed each time. In fact, in his frustration, the king even asks Balaam to refrain from either cursing or blessing the Israelites (Num. 23:25). However, once the process has been set in motion, Balaam is not in control of his message, for he says, "Whatever the LORD says, that is what I must do" (Num. 23:26).

In the end, the Israelites are blessed three times, and an angry Balak rages about, striking his hands together and refusing to pay Balaam's fee. The foreign prophet, known for his ability to speak for the gods and interpret dreams and omens, shrugs this off and simply repeats his disclaimer. The episode concludes with an oracle against Moab, which predicts Israelite rule over all of the Transjordan (Num. 24:10–25). The biblical writers have thus woven the universalism theme into Balaam's insistence on speaking only Yahweh's message. In this way he transcends the normal role of the ancient Near Eastern **diviner,** or servant of the gods, and demonstrates to the Israelites that Yahweh is the only true God.

Rahab and the Siege of Jericho

At the beginning of the conquest narrative in the book of Joshua, the Israelites are faced with their first military test at Jericho, the major oasis site just north of the Dead Sea. This strategic point dominated the entrance into central Palestine and was a natural target for the invaders (note its use by Moabite conquerors in Judg. 3:13). The narrative reinforces Joshua's right to lead the people as Moses' successor by staging several miraculous events that closely parallel events in Moses' career. Thus, as the people prepare to cross the Jordan River, Joshua is instructed by God to line up the tribes in a grand procession led by Levites carrying the ark of the covenant (Josh. 3:3–6). When they reach the river, it is in flood stage (symbolic of chaos' attempt to forestall creation—Gen. 1:1–2 and Marduk's battle with Tiamat in the *Enuma Elish*). However, the Levites are told to confidently step forward into the water, and it rolls back on either side so that the Israelites can pass through on dry land (Josh. 3:14–17), just as they passed through the Red Sea under Moses' direction (Ex. 14:21–22).

Having reestablished both Joshua's leadership role and Yahweh's control over the forces of nature, the tribes move on toward Jericho. The writers of Joshua create a narrative filled with confidence in the ability of the Israelites to take the land with God's help (save only for the story of Achan in Josh. 7). The chapters are filled with the exploits of enthusiastic warriors who follow Joshua without question (the one major difference between the stories of Moses and Joshua). The storytellers also demonstrate the certainty of success by portraying non-Israelites as witnesses to Yahweh's accomplishments. In this way they introduce the universalism theme.

The choice of the prostitute Rahab as the means of advancing the claim of Yahweh's universal authority seems odd at first.

She is a **liminal** character, working in a profession that deprives her of the status of wife or honored widow; Rahab stands outside normal categories for women of her time. Certainly, she could serve as a source of information for Joshua's spies (Josh. 2:1b), but surely other groups within Jericho might be approached—persons with higher status. However, the image created for the Israelites in these stories is of an escaped group of slaves. Their own status while they were in Egypt could not have been any lower than Rahab's, and, therefore, in their national epics they were sympathetic to the "underdog" and to the weak (see Deut. 15:12–15; 24:17–18).

What the spies might not have expected, however, was Rahab's ability to set aside her natural loyalties to her people and her gods. Some have speculated that this was simply a reflection of an oppressed member of the lower class who took the opportunity to join the winning side in a war. But the biblical writers make it clear that Rahab's discernment of God's manifest abilities is the basis for her conversion. As she bargains for the lives of her family, Rahab makes the one argument that the Israelites cannot ignore:

> I know that the Lord has given you the land, and that dread of you has fallen on us, and that all the inhabitants of the land melt in fear before you. For we have heard how the Lord dried up the water of the Red Sea before you when you came out of Egypt, and what you did to the two kings of the Amorites that were beyond the Jordan, to Sihon and Og, whom you utterly destroyed...The Lord your God is indeed God in heaven above and on earth below. (Josh. 2:9–11)

In the biblical narrative prior to Rahab, only Abraham uses this expression that acknowledges Yahweh's lordship over heaven and earth (Gen. 24:3). It is found in Deuteronomy 4:35, 39, but these passages date to the sixth century B.C.E. or later and are part of the movement toward monotheism within Judaism in the postexilic period. Certainly, it is possible that the Deuteronomist (the composite voice associated with the books from Joshua to 2 Kings) has placed this statement in Rahab's mouth. What matters, however, is the artistry with which the biblical writers make their case for Yahweh's position using this theme.

Completing Rahab's story is another example of the remnant theme. The city of Jericho had been placed under the law of *herem* and thus was subject to complete destruction as a sacrifice to God. Rahab's statement of faith marks her as a righteous person. The result, based on what has been discussed in the chapter on remnant, is that she and her family cannot be killed indiscriminately in the general massacre of her people. As a result, the spies take an oath to protect her and her family (Josh. 2:13) if she marks her residence with a red cord (2:17–21, a clear parallel with the marking of the Israelite houses during the Passover). Only in this way are their lives spared from what would otherwise be a mandatory sacrifice. As always, justice is more important to God than sacrifice (see 1 Sam. 15:22; Am. 5:21–24).

Na'aman and Elisha

Embedded within a series of stories involving the prophet Elisha is the tale of Na'aman the Syrian general. Like Rahab, Na'aman is a liminal person. Contracting leprosy has socially neutralized this high-status individual, an avowed enemy of Israel. He can no longer perform his normal military tasks, and he cannot approach his king or serve as an adviser. In his desperation to recapture his health and his role in society, Na'aman takes a chance by listening to the advice of an Israelite slave girl in his household. She tells him to consult the prophet in Samaria for a cure. Given no real options, the general, and by extension his country and gods, must seek the help of Israel and its God (see the reverse situation in king Ahaziah's attempt to consult the Philistine god Baal-zebub in 2 Kings 1:2–4).

A certain amount of diplomatic discussion is necessary to grant Na'aman safe conduct through Israelite territory. The unnamed king of Israel, presumably one of Ahab's sons, does not even consider consulting Elisha or God about the matter. He goes into mourning, seeing the request as a provocative act on the part of the Syrians, who obviously wish to create an incident that will spark a war between them (2 Kings 5:5–7). Elisha must therefore rescue both Na'aman from his disease and the king of Israel from his despair (5:8).

Undoubtedly, the king was relieved to be able to pass this problem on to Elisha. It was now up to the Syrian general to complete his quest and then go home. Na'aman had brought a large entourage with him as well as a huge treasure to pay for his cure (5:5). He operated under the assumption that important persons required complicated cures and that the more one paid for it the better the cure would be. He also expected a spectacular set of actions by the prophet, with hands waved mysteriously over the affected areas and solemn rituals performed in the name of the God, as justification for the expense (5:11). None of his expectations were fulfilled.

Elisha makes no effort to grant the general an audience or to speak with him in person. Instead, a servant relays the message that Na'aman need only go down to the Jordan River and wash himself in its waters seven times to be cured of his leprosy (5:10).

But no one wants to go to the doctor and only speak with the receptionist. A high-status person expects the deference due his rank, and in any case, "Are not...the rivers of Damascus better than all the waters of Israel?" (5:12).

Na'aman's pride almost costs him his cure. However, he is eventually convinced by members of his party to carry out the prophet's instructions. Miraculously, he is cured and he is beside himself with joy (5:13–14). Once again, a statement of faith comes from the lips of a non-Israelite. Na'aman expresses a sense of awareness that never seems to be found (at least according to the prophets) in the mouth of an Israelite: "Now I know that there is no God in all the earth except in Israel" (5:15).

Curiously, the general also asks for two mule-loads of dirt so that he can take it back to Syria with him and construct an altar. He believes that Yahweh's presence must be physically transported to his country in order to make sacrifices to the one God who truly responds to his needs. This understanding of the localization of divine presence is an indication of the originality of this story. Instead of simply placing words into the mouth of a character that reinforces the Yahwist theology, the reader is confronted with an ancient belief system that can accommodate itself to new understandings of the gods. Na'aman has been presented with the truth of Yahweh's power, and he vows that he will "no longer offer burnt offering or sacrifice to any god except the LORD" (5:17).

Just because Na'aman has acknowledged Yahweh as the God to whom he will now give his devotion does not mean that he can ignore the social conventions of his own country. The political realities of Na'aman's world are also made evident in his request that the prophet absolve him from any hint of idolatry when he performs his official duties for the king of Syria. This includes a ritual in the temple of their god Rimmon, in which he bows before the image of the god. Na'aman declares that he knows the difference between true worship and ritual practice, and he asks to be forgiven for an act that now has social rather than religious significance to him (5:18). Elisha's statement that he depart "in peace" suggests that the path to monotheism does require some compromise.

Postexilic Expressions of Universalism

The transformation of Israelite religion into Judaism takes a major step in the postexilic period (between 500–200 B.C.E.). The Babylonian conquest of Judah in 587 B.C.E. had eliminated the monarchy, the temple in Jerusalem, and the city of Jerusalem itself as a political capital. A large proportion of the population had been deported, starting with the Assyrian period in 721 B.C.E. and continuing to 586 B.C.E., leaving the land of Judah without the leadership and integrated economy that had made it a viable country. As a result, the basis for a new cultural identity had to be forged in the wilderness of exile (see a full discussion of this in the chapter on remnant). In addition, the prospect and the reality of return from exile divided the Israelite people between those in Palestine and those who remained in the diaspora, all the scattered lands of exile.

The universalism theme continues to be a part of the writings from this late period, but instead of a didactic tool to convince the Israelites to obey the covenant and worship only Yahweh, it takes on the further dimension of demonstrating to other nations the power of Israel's God. In some instances, it also functions as an argument against the growing tendency within the Jewish community to become exclusivistic. So, for example, the postexilic voice of Isaiah argues that even eunuchs and "foreigners," or **proselytes**, have a full place within the community if they keep the Sabbath and "hold fast" to the covenant (Isa. 56:1–8). The Jewish Identity Movement (see the remnant chapter) had helped save the exiles from **assimilation** and cultural oblivion during the exile. However, it had also reinforced the idea of a chosen people, built barriers against intermarriage with other groups (Ezra 9:1–3), and established rules of ritual purity that restricted access to temple worship and full membership in the Jewish community (Deut. 23:1–3; Lev. 21:17–21). The universalism theme in the postexilic period now takes on the task of allowing Yahweh to be a God concerned with all nations.

Cyrus and Isaiah of the Exile

The end of the Babylonian exile brought great changes for the community of exiles from Judah. The Persians, under King Cyrus, defeated the Neo-Babylonian armies throughout their empire and finally laid siege to Babylon itself in 540 B.C.E. According to the decree issued by Cyrus, he was aided in his campaign against Babylon's king Nabonidus by Babylon's patron deity, Marduk (compare with the Assyrian claim during the siege of Jerusalem in 2 Kings 18:22–25). As part of the Persian plan to reorganize their new territories, Cyrus ordered that funds be set aside to help rebuild the temples of the gods that had been held hostage in Babylon. In addition, those exiled peoples who had settled in Mesopotamia were now free to return to their homelands.

Within the exilic community there existed a group, or school, dedicated to the ideas and prophecies of Isaiah of Jerusalem. They saw the transition of political masters as a fulfillment of Jeremiah's prophecy that God would eventually return them to their place (Jer. 29:10–14). But they also realized that they would have to seize the opportunity to use Cyrus' victory to herald Yahweh's manipulation of these events. The Persian king had employed his own spin, or theodicy, on his successes, claiming that Marduk had searched the world for a "righteous ruler" to restore proper worship of the god in Babylon. Marduk had chosen Cyrus because of his "good deeds and upright heart."

The revived voice of Isaiah, perhaps having heard Cyrus' decree or seen a copy displayed for the public, wants to assure his own people that the God responsible for Cyrus' great victory and their liberation is Yahweh, not Marduk. In doing so, he follows part of the outline of Cyrus' statement, but makes it clear who is really God:

> Thus says the LORD to his anointed, to Cyrus, whose right hand I have grasped to subdue nations before him and strip kings of their robes, to open doors before him—and the gates shall not be closed...so that you may know that it is I, the LORD, the God of Israel, who call you by your name. For the sake of my servant Jacob, and Israel my chosen, I call you by your name, I surname you, though you do not know me. I am the LORD, and there is no other; besides me there is no god. (Isa. 45:1–5)

Note the parallels here. First, both Marduk and Yahweh have named Cyrus as their champion. They each consider him worthy of favor. Both have given him a victory by "opening doors" (a physical reality, since the priests of Marduk open Babylon's gates to the Persian troops). Finally, both have lent divine sanction to a king who previously had not been an adherent of that god.

It does not matter to the Isaiah voice that Cyrus is unaware of Yahweh's actions. All that really matters is that the exiles know that God has once again chosen a tool to affect historical events (compare with Isa. 10:5). What is distinctive about this narrative is the use of the title "anointed," or **messiah,** for Cyrus. No other non-Israelite ruler is given this honor, and it stands as a testament to the importance that is placed on this event—a new release from bondage, a new exodus. Although Cyrus will not become a new Moses figure, his political stature as the ruler of the largest empire in all the history of the ancient Near East to that time is drawn upon by the prophet as a parallel to Yahweh's universal authority. Quite simply, Cyrus' rise to power is God's means of letting all nations know "from the rising of the sun and from the west, that there is no one besides me; I am the LORD, and there is no other" (Isa. 45:6).

Jonah and the Lesson of Universalism

The tensions created in the postexilic period by the desire to enforce Jewish identity through exclusivistic claims and cultural isolation also lead to a voice within the biblical text calling for a wider understanding of Yahweh's concerns for creation. In the story of Jonah, the author uses the familiar tool of humor to get the point across that Yahweh is concerned about peoples other than Israel. Jonah becomes a lightning rod attracting God's attention and drawing other people into an awareness of Yahweh's power. The story shows that the prophet, like the people, has to be persuaded that there is no such thing as "undeserved" forgiveness.

The story begins with an outrageous mission. Jonah is instructed to go to Nineveh, the hated capital city of the Assyrians, and provide the people there with the same sort of warning offered by other Hebrew prophets to their own people. God's statement, "their wickedness has come up before me" (Jon. 1:2) is reminiscent of the prelude to the flood (Gen. 6:5) and the concern expressed over the evil of Sodom and Gomorrah (Gen. 18:20–21). In that sense, the instruction given to Jonah simply follows previous examples of the remnant theme. The Assyrians, as part of God's creation, must be given the opportunity to repent, lest God be placed in a situation in which a righteous person is destroyed without warning.

As the narrative progresses, it seems that everyone is willing to accept God's help except Jonah. When the prophet flees his country, his ship is threatened by a storm. All the sailors are madly throwing cargo overboard and praying to their own gods. Only Jonah does nothing. He is asleep in the hold and only comes on deck when the sailors rouse him with the plea to add his prayers to their own. They hope that attracting yet another god's attention will still the sea (Jon. 1:5–6). Then, when they take the further step of casting lots to determine the cause of their misfortune (compare with Josh. 7:16–20), Jonah has to admit that the fault is his. The sailors cannot believe that anyone could be foolish enough to try to flee from a god, but they take Jonah's advice and cast him into the sea. Then they pray to Yahweh, offer a sacrifice, and take vows—another example of the use of non-Israelites who discern the power of the Israelite God (Jon. 1:14–16).

After spending three days reconsidering his refusal to obey God's command, Jonah miraculously finds himself outside the walls of Nineveh. The fish (1:17; 2:10) and the storm function in the story as evidence of God's control over the natural world. In a way, they parallel the whirlwind in Job that serves to divide the mortal from the divine sphere of authority (Job 38:1). As a result of his adventure, Jonah is confronted with the inescapability of the prophetic call and now, still reluctantly, enters the Assyrian city.

At this point Jonah becomes the most successful prophet of all time. His very simple message, "Forty days more, and Nineveh shall be overthrown" (Jon. 3:4) immediately convinces the people of Nineveh. They express their belief in Yahweh and put on **sackcloth** to show their willingness to mourn for their past evil. The Assyrian king becomes a model of repentance (compare with King Ahab in 1 Kings 21:27–29) and decrees a fast for all his subjects, including their animals. In fact, even the animals are clothed in sackcloth (despite the action's comic overtones) to prove to God that the whole nation repents of its evil (Jon. 3:6–8). Ironically, the justification given for these extreme measures is the same as in the trial of Jeremiah. The prophet had prophesied against the city of Jerusalem just as Micah had one hundred years before. The elders hoped that God would relent if they released him unharmed:

> Who knows? God may relent and change his mind; he may turn from his fierce anger, so that we do not perish. (Jon. 3:9)

> Did King Hezekiah of Judah and all Judah actually put him [Micah] to death? Did he not fear the LORD and entreat the favor of the LORD, and did not the LORD change his mind about the disaster that he had pronounced against them? But we are about to bring great disaster on ourselves! (Jer. 26:19)

By their actions, the Assyrians save themselves and their city, but Jonah is not happy (Jon. 4:1). He complains that God is too kindhearted and prone to forgiveness. The Assyrians have been responsible for terrible acts of destruction against the peoples of the Near East, and now God has forgiven them! The prophet is so beside himself over this that he asks for God to take his life (4:3).

Now, at last, the author of the story has brought his audience to the point of the entire narrative. When Jonah complains about the death of the bush that has been giving him shade from the heat of the day and once again calls on God to allow him to die, the prophet sets himself and his people up for the climax (4:7–8). God, speaking to Jonah in much the same way as Yahweh does to Job (Job 38–41), puts the shortsighted prophet in his place. God points out that Jonah has had nothing to do with the creation of the bush or of the people of Nineveh. He therefore has no right to deny the creator the opportunity to be concerned with them (Jon. 4:10–11). In other words, God asserts sovereignty and compassionate concern for all creation, a full expression of the universalism theme.

Wisdom and the Lesson of Universalism

Although the wisdom theme will be discussed in depth in another chapter, it is worth noting here how the universalism theme is employed in this **genre** of biblical literature. Wisdom involves "right behavior" as well as "right thinking." Thus, a wise person is one who has the knowledge of God and is capable of acting on that knowledge to perform acceptable worship practices and to be obedient to the stipulations of the covenant found in the law (Ps. 1). A negative example of this expectation is found in Hosea's charge against the Israelites that they "are destroyed for lack of knowledge" (Hos. 4:6).

It thus becomes the purpose of wisdom literature in the Bible to provide the knowledge necessary for the people of the covenant to become God's obedient servants. Like the prophets who warn the people so that the righteous remnant may hear and act to ensure their survival in the face of God's punishment, the wisdom author wants to prevent the people from coming to ruin for lack of understanding (Hos. 4:14).

Attendant to this knowledge of God's law and the covenant agreement is a further understanding of the universality of God's domain and power. The Psalms have a number of examples of the infinite nature of God as creator and provider:

> O LORD, our Sovereign, how majestic is your name in all the earth! You have set your glory above the heavens. (Ps. 8:1)

> The heavens are telling the glory of God; and the firmament proclaims his handiwork. Day to day pours forth speech, and night to night declares knowledge. There is no speech, nor are there words; their voice is not heard; yet their voice goes out through all the earth, and their words to the end of the world. (Ps. 19:1–4)

> Let all the earth fear the LORD; let all the inhabitants of the world stand in awe of him. For he spoke, and it came to be; he commanded, and it stood firm. (Ps. 33:8–9)

Each of these expressions of praise expands the realm of Yahweh far beyond Israel, encompassing all of creation.

Job and Universalism

The author of the book of Job draws once again on a non-Israelite character to express the universalism theme. Job is a well-known wisdom character, usually associated with the land of Edom (Uz), who is described as a righteous man. The basis for the claim that he is upright is summarized in the statement that he "feared God and turned away from evil" (Job 1:1), and he made sacrifices even for his children in case they might have sinned "in their hearts" (1:5). There is no mention of either the Abrahamic or Mosaic covenant in the book, because Job is not an Israelite. And yet he is set as a model of behavior in Ezekiel (14:14, 20) along with two other non-Israelites—Noah and Daniel (possibly the Danil of the Ugaritic Aqhat Epic or some other Near Eastern sage). This is repeated in the Deuterocanonical literature (Sir. 49:9). What seems likely, therefore, is that the biblical writer of Job is making the case, as Ezekiel did, for the existence of righteous persons outside the covenant community. They too can be upright, and they too can come to the knowledge of Yahweh as the universal God.

The premise throughout Job is that Yahweh is the only power in the universe. No other god is ever mentioned, and there is no hint that any force in the cosmos may challenge God's supreme power. In a way, this makes Job's miserable condition that much more difficult for him. Because he has no other god or advocate to turn to in his plight, he is forced to ask God continually to give him a sign or appear before him to explain why the righteous must suffer (Job 9:15–24; 23:3–5). He knows the source of his punishment, but does not know why he is made to suffer in front of those who had previously respected him (12:4). This does not prevent Job from freely acknowledging God's attributes:

> With God are wisdom and strength; he has counsel and understanding. If he tears down, no one can rebuild; if he shuts someone in, no one can open up. (Job 12:13–14)

> By his power he stilled the Sea; by his understanding he struck down Rahab. By his wind the heavens were made fair; his hand pierced the fleeing serpent. These are indeed but the outskirts of his ways; and how small a whisper do we hear of him! But the thunder of his power who can understand? (Job 26:12–14)

Job's plight goes to the heart of the question of the relationship between the human and the divine (see Ps. 8:3–8). Is it possible for mortals to fully understand the mind of God? Is there a form of knowledge available that will bring humans to the same plateau of power where God dwells? Job believes in the universal qualities of Yahweh, but he does not understand the purpose of an existence filled with loss and pain. This confusion becomes even more graphic when he recites his "oath of clearance" in chapter 31. He is able to chronicle all the possible sins he could have committed, and yet he is able to say, with a clear conscience, that he knows he is innocent.

Ultimately, when God does appear before Job, the mortal is confronted with the reality of divine power (Job 38–39). Job, who thought he knew God, is forced to endure Yahweh's harsh questioning, which is entirely designed to demonstrate how little, on a divine scale, the mortal actually does know. Again, it is a universal God who puts Job in his place. The writer emphasizes the singular majesty of a deity who did lay "the foundation of the earth" (38:4) and knows "the ordinances of the heavens" (38:33). Job's final response, repenting of his proud claims to knowledge, leaves no doubt about who is the sole, all-powerful God (42:2–6).

Job's story completes the development of the universalism theme. The theme had started as a means of discerning Yahweh's power among the range of other gods and as a didactic tool of the biblical storytellers to convince the Israelites which God they should worship. The "contests between gods" motif allowed a case to be made for Yahweh's sovereign power. The creation and flood epics also contributed to the understanding of Yahweh as a transcendent deity capable of performing all the acts attributed to the host of other gods. Bringing non-Israelites into the narrative also advanced the universalism theme through their statements of faith. This provided conclusive and "neutral" witness to the reality of Yahweh's universal powers. Finally, in wisdom literature and the book of Job, the biblical writers bring their argument to culmination as they tell of a universe entirely in the hands of God, with no mention whatsoever of other divine forces.

CHAPTER 4

Wisdom

One of the common misconceptions that readers of the Bible have about wisdom literature is that it is limited to Proverbs, Ecclesiastes, and Job. The genre of wisdom actually permeates the entire Old Testament. Certainly, it is to be found in wisdom sayings or dialogues, philosophical discussions, and examinations of the nature of the universe. However, it is also built into the very structure of ancient Israelite society. Religious rituals and social expectations are both centered on "right behavior" and "right thinking." To act in a manner considered by one's society as proper or appropriate brings honor to that person and to his or her household. Deviations, both large and small, from the expected norms in speech, dress, or action bring shame, embarrassment, and sanction against individuals and households.

Wisdom, therefore, is an expression of both the common sense and the moral tone of a society. Aphorisms, laws, and the official chronicle of events in a king's reign all reflect the basic attitudes about correct behavior and speech. This theme is so pervasive, in fact, that it would be difficult to separate the wisdom characteristics from any portion of the biblical text. They are simply a natural part of the composition process. As such, they are some of the most valuable cultural artifacts available for the reconstruction of life in ancient society.

Characteristics of the Wisdom Theme

- Strong emphasis on an established moral or social code of conduct
- Concern with the question of good and evil in the world
- A glorification of God as creator and source of all true knowledge
- A measure of honor and shame within society

Wisdom in the Ancient Near East

Before examining wisdom as a theme in the biblical text, it is necessary to begin with a brief survey of wisdom literature in the ancient Near East. Several pieces of Egyptian and Mesopotamian wisdom literature contain close parallels with the book of Proverbs and provide a foundation for wisdom in the rest of the Old Testament. Among the texts recovered from Egypt are the "Teachings of Ptah-hotep" (ca. 2500 B.C.E.), the "Protests of the Eloquent Peasant" (ca. 2000 B.C.E.), the "Teachings of Amen-em-ope" (ca. 1200 B.C.E.), and the "Teachings of Ankhsheshonqy" (ca. 200 B.C.E.). Valuable material can also be found in the "Memphite Theology of Creation" (ca. 2200 B.C.E.) and the "Dispute over Suicide" (ca. 2000 B.C.E.). Additional proverbial sayings and examples of traditional behavior are in the Assyrian "Teachings of Ahiqar" (ca. 700 B.C.E.), and in the Ugaritic epics of Ba'al and Anat and of the ancient heroes Keret and Aqhat (ca. 1400 B.C.E.). These and other texts will be drawn on throughout this chapter to demonstrate the common literary and cultural milieu of the ancient Near East.

Comparisons that are drawn between these pieces of wisdom literature and the biblical text can be attributed to the universality of wisdom sayings. It was very common in the ancient world for poets, sages, and scribes to borrow phrases or even entire episodes or stories. Some cultural adjustments had to be made, but the physical context and social norms were similar enough that it was natural to incorporate foreign ideas or stories that spoke to one's own people. Here are some examples:

Adultery:

> But he who commits adultery has no sense; he who does it destroys himself. He will get wounds and dishonor, and his disgrace will not be wiped away. For jealousy arouses a husband's fury, and he shows no restraint when he takes revenge. (Prov. 6:32–34)

> If you become the father of a household or are a houseguest, stay away from the women of the house. Keep your mind on business, your eyes off pretty faces. Foolish dreamers become casualties of unwise actions. ("Teachings of Ptah-hotep," *OTP*, p. 268)

> A man who makes love to a married woman will be executed on her threshold. ("Teachings of Ankhsheshonqy," *OTP*, p. 294)

"Better is" motif:

> Better is a little with the fear of the LORD than great treasure and trouble with it. Better is a dinner of vegetables where love is than a fatted ox and hatred with it. (Prov. 15:16–17)

> Better a single loaf and a happy heart than all the riches in the world and sorrow. ("Teachings of Amen-em-ope," *OTP*, p. 277)

> Better to dwell in your own house than in someone else's mansion. ("Teachings of Ankhsheshonqy," *OTP*, p. 294)

Another favorite device of wisdom writers in the ancient Near East is the progression pattern (note its use in prophetic speech in Amos 1–2). So, for instance, in the Assyrian sage Ahiqar's teachings, he says that "two kinds of people are a delight, a third pleases Shamash: those who share their wine, those who follow good advice, and those who can keep secrets" (*OTP*, p. 284). Taking a negative tack, the wisdom writer in Proverbs 6:16–19 notes "six things that the Lord hates, seven that are an abomination to him." The author of Ecclesiastes 11:2 takes a cautious view of business and uses the pattern to advise a merchant to divide his investments "seven ways, or even eight" to plan for expected losses.

The universality of wisdom sayings and situations is also made evident in ancient epic narrative. One example is an episode of the Gilgamesh Epic from ancient Mesopotamia. The hero has just watched his friend, Enkidu, die a slow and painful death, and Gilgamesh resolves to go on a quest to find the secret of immortality so that he may escape a similar fate. His journey will eventually take him to the Eden-like land of Dilmun. But on the way he encounters Siduri, a tavern maid, with whom he discusses his plan to become immortal. In one version of the story, Siduri advises Gilgamesh to give up his quest for immortality and return home to enjoy what life offers to mortals. She tells him:

> Let your belly be full, make merry day and night.
> Turn each day into a feast of rejoicing. Dance and
> play day and night. Put on fresh garments. Wash
> your hair and body clean in water. Play with your
> children. Take pleasure in your wife. (*OTP*, p. 24)

The hero is not willing to take this advice and resumes his journey, one fated ultimately to fail because the gods seldom share their immortal state with humans. Siduri's prescription for mortal existence is remarkably similar to an admonition in Ecclesiastes:

> I know that there is nothing better for them than
> to be happy and enjoy themselves as long as they
> live; moreover, it is God's gift that all should eat
> and drink and take pleasure in all their toil. (Eccl.
> 3:12–13)

In fact, the idyllic life for the ancients is one of peace in which landowners can "sit under their own vines and under their own fig trees" (Mic. 4:4; see also 2 Kings 18:31 and Zech. 3:10). The specter of premature death and suffering was a constant companion for these ancient peoples (Job 7:1–6), and so it is not surprising that they would see common sense in living in the present and enjoying every day as it comes.

Only in Egyptian literature is death considered a comfort, but the Egyptians were the only ancient culture to develop a clear sense of the afterlife as a continuation of one's earthly existence. In the "Dispute over Suicide," a despondent man argues with his soul that life is no longer worth living. In the hope of achieving an end to his misery, the man begs his soul to accompany him into the afterlife and notes that "life is only a transition. Even trees fall" (*OTP*, p. 209). Ultimately, however, the soul makes the most telling point in the debate and apparently wins the argument:

> Throw your cares on the fire with your offerings, get on with your life…Stop thinking about dying. When it is time for you to die…then I will travel with you. Then we shall live together forever. (*OTP*, pp. 213–14)

From these and many other examples of wisdom literature, as well as their own life experiences, the ancient Israelites formed their own understanding of right behavior. Every culture learns that survival is based on basic civility and honesty, as well as on vigilance against one's enemies. Thus, the Israelites could see, like the Egyptian sage Amen-em-ope, that there was value to treating the poor fairly. And like the Assyrian Ahiqar, they saw the wisdom in honoring one's parents:

- Do not steal from the poor…Do not abuse the elderly …Do not conspire to defraud anyone…Do not sue those who wrong you… ("Amen-em-ope,"*OTP*, p. 275)
- Do not rob the poor because they are poor, or crush the afflicted at the gate. (Prov. 22:22)
- Those who do not honor their parent's name are cursed for their evil by Shamash, the divine judge. (*OTP*, p. 287)
- Honor your father and your mother, so that your days may be long in the land that the LORD your God is giving you. (Ex. 20:12)

Wisdom as a Guide to Behavior

If wisdom was to serve as a guide to behavior in ancient Israelite society, it had to be used to determine what they considered to be "right thought," "right speech," and "right action." In the discussion that follows, examples are drawn from the text to provide examples of each of these concepts. In some cases, they are simple expressions of good advice or common sense. In some examples from the narrative passages the characters and the audience must both analyze right behavior.

One way of beginning this examination of the text is with the model provided in Psalm 1. This wisdom psalm clearly defines the difference between the wise person and the fool, two categories that are also found in Mesopotamian and Egyptian wisdom literature. Psalm 1 points to the proper way of life and the dangers of association with the foolish:

> Happy are those who do not follow the advice of the wicked, or take the path that sinners tread, or sit in the seat of the scoffers; but their delight is in the law of the Lord, and on his law they meditate day and night. (Ps. 1:1–2)

The comparison between the wise person and the fool is a common theme in the wisdom literature of the ancient Near East. One task of wisdom is to reassure the people that evil or foolish behavior will not be rewarded. Thus, in the Egyptian teachings of Ptah-hotep (ca. twenty-fifth century B.C.E.) the sage expresses the proper attitude about work: "The wise rise early to start to work, but fools rise early to worry about all there is to do." The ability to make one's way in society without causing undue harm or distress is described in a saying by the Egyptian sage Amen-em-ope (ca. eleventh century B.C.E.): "More dangerous are the words of fools than storm winds on open water." Another Egyptian teacher, Ankhsheshonqy (ca. third century B.C.E.), notes that "a wise man seeks friends, and a fool seeks enemies." In each of these statements, the wisdom tradition makes it clear that a retribution principle operates in the universe that balances the harm caused by unthinking words and actions with the healing words and actions of the wise or righteous person.

Progression from "Right Thought" to "Right Action"

It is difficult to separate the various aspects of wisdom-inspired behavior. No proper behavior is possible without "right thought," which leads to "right speech" and "right action." Throughout ancient Near Eastern wisdom literature, "right thought" is the quality of the cool-headed person. In Egyptian wisdom literature, Amen-em-ope advises the wise person to "stop and think before you speak" (*OTP*, p. 276). Those who rush in without due deliberation are the "fools" who come to disaster. Of course, for rational decisions to be made, the wise person must also study a situation, gather facts, and seek sound advice. The thought process is therefore more than a pause before action. It is a deliberate process, based on reasoned and informed thinking. So the author of Proverbs can state with confidence that "the upright give thought to their ways" (Prov. 21:29).

Perhaps one of the best places to look for the progression from thought to action is found in Psalm 10. In this **lament**, the psalmist is discouraged by the apparent success enjoyed by the wicked and points out what he considers their unwise path. They begin their foolish journey by convincing themselves that "there is no God" (10:4). This then gives them the confidence to speak curses, deceit, and mischief (10:7). Finally, feeling invulnerable to authority, "they lurk in secret like a lion…that they may seize the poor" (10:9), while continually reminding themselves that God "will never see it" (10:11).

It is exactly this type of self-delusion that stands at the heart of Jeremiah's complaint against the people of Jerusalem, who commit acts of murder, theft, adultery, and idolatry and then come to the temple and assume that their ritual acts make them "safe" (Jer. 7:9–10). The prophet is hoping to break through to those who are willing to take advice from the wise (Prov. 12:15), but like the Egyptian sage Ankhsheshonqy, Jeremiah knows that the most common response when one attempts to instruct a fool is hatred of the instructor (*OTP*, p. 289; Prov. 23:9).

The biblical narrative contains several stories in which the failure to think before speaking and the inability to take sound advice or listen to reason leads to disaster. One of the best examples is found in the story of David, Nabal, and Abigail in

1 Samuel 25. The name of the villain of the piece provides a clue to its "wisdom" content. Since Nabal is the Hebrew word for "fool," the audience immediately is prepared to be instructed in right behavior with Nabal as the negative example. They know that "the wise of heart will heed commandments, but a babbling fool will come to ruin" (Prov. 10:8).

Like most biblical stories, this one operates on several levels, and it should be understood that it also forms part of a narrative designed to justify David's rise to the throne of Israel, replacing King Saul's family. Presumably, Nabal is a political supporter of Saul. David and his men had been forced into an "outlaw" existence (probably the model for the Robin Hood **legend** of medieval England). To survive and to gain support from some of the influential landowners in Judah, David instructed his men to protect the flocks and herdsmen of the southern hill country. In return, they asked that the owners provide them with the supplies they needed. This is exactly what they had done for Nabal and his men, but when they requested "payment" for their services, Nabal, without thinking, refused to acknowledge any debt owed to men "who are breaking away from their masters" (1 Sam. 25:10–11).

In essence, he failed to uphold the honor of his household in dealing with David on a feast day when he should have played the gracious host (25:6–11). If it was his political tie to Saul that stood in his way, this could have been explained diplomatically without shaming David and implying that David had no household or personal honor: "Who is David? Who is the son Jesse?" (25:10). However, he turned David's messengers away as if they were bandits or beggars.

By doing this, Nabal violated one of the cardinal tenets of Near Eastern tradition, the law of reciprocity. It was inexcusable for him to have received a service or a gift, benefited from it, and then failed to reciprocate in kind. In the wisdom literature of the ancient Near East, it is made quite clear that the head of a household may obtain honor through his generosity. For instance, in the Egyptian "Teachings of Ptah-hotep," the sage states that if you obtain a position of authority, you should "be generous with the wealth that the gods give you and take care of your hometown now that you can" (*OTP*, p. 269). Similarly, the

Egyptian wisdom of Amen-em-ope cautions that it is "better to be praised for loving your neighbor than loving your wealth" (*OTP*, p. 280).

The Protocol of Reciprocity

1. Gifts must be given by a patron for every service rendered by a client.
2. All gifts must be of equal value so that there is no advantage to be gained by either side of the exchange.
3. Failure to give an appropriate gift dishonors the donor and insults the recipient.
4. The recipient may not contest the gift offered. The gift may only be refused if there is a question of dishonor or imbalance.

Traditional societies, such as those that existed in the ancient Near East, gauge themselves and their symbolic identities on the ability to achieve personal and group honor and avoid shame. As the author of Proverbs notes, "the wise will inherit honor, but stubborn fools, disgrace" (3:35). One way that honor is obtained is through the ritualized exchange of presents or services. The law of reciprocity was designed to enhance prestige and to protect one's household. Generosity brought honor to both the one who gave a gift and to the recipient of the gift (Prov. 19:6). But Nabal had refused to acknowledge any debt to David, had insulted him, and had in effect challenged David's "household" to a contest of survival.

David's response is therefore obligatory and a model of proper behavior. As Israel's future king and a head of a threatened household, he cannot allow Nabal's foolish and antisocial behavior to triumph. As a result, David takes a vow to completely destroy Nabal's household (1 Sam. 25:22). Nabal's improper speech and inappropriate action have unleashed the forces of destruction. But a good wisdom story cannot end with such a dismal prospect. Thus, Nabal's wife, Abigail, steps forward to become the wisdom figure in the narrative and save, through her proper speech and appropriate action, her household.

Abigail, if she is to save her household from the foolish actions of her husband, must act swiftly and courageously. She decides to use the same strategy employed by Jacob when he returned to Canaan and met his brother Esau (Gen. 32:3–21). Abigail sends messengers who bring gifts to David before she arrives in his camp. Her appeal to David then includes the following reasoned arguments:

1. **Respect for a Patron:** She makes obeisance to David, acknowledging his leadership as "chief," and calls him to place the guilt for what has happened on her head alone (compare with similar statements in Gen. 27:13 and 2 Sam. 14:9). This deflects his anger to a different target and allows a pause for reflection on his course of action. It also reverses the power relationship. David had appealed to Nabal as a client who had done a service for his patron. Now Abigail treats David as if her household were his client.

2. **Cites Mitigating Circumstances:** She excuses her husband's actions, using the appeal to wisdom, saying that this is just what would be expected of an "ill-natured fellow" (i.e., fools should not be taken seriously, and others should not be forced to pay for their ill-conceived actions—Prov. 26:2; Sir. 27:27). It also is indicative of her political action of acknowledging the lordship of David's household, an act comparable to the bride's shift in loyalties at the time of the betrothal (see Rebekah's actions in Gen. 24:55–59).

3. **Justifies Offer of Hospitality:** Although the male head of household has the right to offer hospitality (Gen. 18:2–5), Abigail asserts her right as "mother" of the household to distribute food, which she would have done had she been present at the time David's messengers had come (1 Sam. 25:25).

4. **Makes Appeal to Wisdom:** She asserts that it was Yahweh who caused David to refrain from shedding innocent blood, thereby demonstrating the true difference between a wise man like David and a fool like Nabal.

5. **Prediction**: Offering food as tribute to God's rightful ruler, Abigail predicts God's providential care of David's person against his enemies and assures David that he will be relieved when he becomes king that he has not been guilty of shedding blood "without cause" (1 Sam. 25:31; compare with Jer. 26:15). The true, divinely ordained ruler recognizes the proper course of action, weighs immediate gratification against true justice, and demonstrates the caution typical of the wise (Prov. 14:15–16).

David responds to Abigail's argument by acknowledging her wise advice. Once again it is a sign of the wise that they discern the difference between the "talk of fools" and sound reasoning (Prov. 14:3). By making a covenant with Abigail, as the representative of her household, David chooses to disregard gender roles. Wisdom is not limited to those in power or to males. As Ptah-hotep, the twenty-fifth century B.C.E. Egyptian sage, notes, the wise person "seeks advice from the powerless, as well as from the powerful," even from "a young woman grinding grain" (*OTP*, p. 266).

Wisdom Arguments

The fact that proper behavior is not always a clear choice can be found in those biblical narratives in which the characters must weigh all the factors before taking action or resolving a dilemma. For example, in Eve's dialogue with the serpent in Genesis 3:1–6, she is faced with a typical wisdom situation. Her curiosity and doubt force her to determine whether she can continue to simply accept God's statement as true or whether she must test its validity. Ultimately, she discovers that there are varieties of truth in this etiological story, which is designed to explain the realities of the human condition. She and Adam do not immediately die after eating from the tree of the knowledge of good and evil. They each gain a new perspective on the world that will give them the opportunity to procreate, invent, and live more self-directed lives. However, the trade-off is the reality that death awaits every human and that life contains both triumph and tragedy.

Job's plight provides another philosophical conundrum. Once again, a truism or proposition is explored through physical experimentation. God asks Satan to "consider" Job, "a blameless and upright man" (Job 1:8). Such an unequivocal statement in a wisdom dialogue requires a test, and "Satan" serves as the means with which God will discover whether "Job fears God for nothing" (1:9–12). Once the experiment begins, Job is perplexed, because according to the rules of his society he is a righteous man (see the universalism chapter). He has performed all the ritual acts normally required and has gone beyond them to protect his children from evil thoughts or unrealized sins (1:5). Then, when he is afflicted with the loss of his children and property and the physical ailments that brand him as a leper (2:7; see Lev. 13:2–16), he attempts to analyze his condition with three "friends." Their arguments and counterarguments center on conventional wisdom and a rather rigid "understanding" of God's justice.

Eliphaz: Argument of Justice and Discipline

- "Who that was innocent ever perished? Or where were the upright cut off?" (4:7)
- "How happy is the one whom God reproves; there fore do not despise the discipline of the Almighty." (5:17)

Bildad: Argument from History and Physical Evidence

- "For inquire now of bygone generations, and consider what their ancestors have found...Will they not teach you and tell you and utter words out of their under standing?" (8:8–10)
- "Surely the light of the wicked is put out...By disease their skin is consumed, the firstborn of Death consumes their limbs." (18:5, 13)

Zophar: Argument of Unquestioning Penitence
- "If you direct your heart rightly, you will stretch out your hands toward him. If iniquity is in your hand, put it far away, and do not let wickedness reside in your tents. Surely then you will lift up your face without blemish." (11:13–15)

Job's responses to these arguments are not always direct, but they do continually assert that he is unaware of any sins (13:23), that humanity's lot is short "and full of trouble" (14:1–2), and that his friends are both "treacherous" and unfeeling in the face of his calamity (6:14–15). He also employs a mechanism known from the Egyptian Book of the Dead to cast aside any charges that he has committed any act against God or his fellow human. In this "Oath of Clearance" (Job 31) he lists sins such as lust, lying, deceit, adultery, abuse of slaves, and failure to give alms to the poor. Each sin is denied, and the punishment that he would have merited for committing them is therefore unjustified.

This treatise on apparently undeserved suffering is only complete when God finally appears to Job (Job 38–41). From a human standpoint, Yahweh's fierce questioning of Job is not very satisfying. Job is forced to admit to his limited powers of understanding and is quite thoroughly put in his place. He is mortal and therefore cannot command God or insist that God perform in a manner that Job believes is proper. This is not to say that God is unjust. Job has committed the sin of hubris, and his excessive pride in his own righteousness and in his supposed knowledge of God has brought him to this draining "final examination."

God only releases Job when he admits that he has spoken "what I did not understand, things too wonderful for me, which I did not know" (42:3). At that point, Job has proven Yahweh's original proposition that he is an upright man "who fears God" (1:8). Job even saves his "friends" from God's anger and is restored to his former prosperity (42:7–10). Proper behavior is thus rewarded, and the equilibrium that has been upset by Job's trial is returned to normal. Job, as the model for every person, has come to the realization stated in the Psalms that "the fear of the LORD is the beginning of wisdom" (Ps. 111:10).

Wisdom Situations

Less philosophical examples of wisdom situations are found in a variety of biblical narratives. Thus, when Joseph is literally backed into a corner by the sexual advances of Potiphar's wife, he must decide who it would be most dangerous to offend. He realizes that as a slave he is virtually powerless to resist her wishes forever, and yet he makes a reasoned argument, based on a code of "right behavior." Joseph cites the heavy responsibilities given to him by his master and the fact that Potiphar has treated Joseph almost as an equal. Therefore, how could Joseph betray that trust by acceding to her demand? This same situation and a similar argument are found in the Egyptian "Tale of Two Brothers."

> When Bata's wife asked Anubis to "lie with her," he was outraged and said, "You and your husband are like a mother and father to me. Because he was older than I, he reared me. How can you possibly suggest I commit a crime like this against him?" *(OTP*, p. 64)

Ultimately, Joseph chooses to accept imprisonment and shame rather than betray his master and the command of his God (Gen. 39:7–20).

In another example from the ancestral narratives, a widow finds herself with no recourse except to deceive her father-in-law and demonstrate through a very risky strategy that the law is on her side (Gen. 38). This story involves Judah and his daughter-in-law Tamar. She was married to Judah's son Er, but he died an untimely death before the couple produced any children. Ordinarily, the law of **levirate obligation** (see Deut. 25:5–10) would guide what was to follow, but a lack of wisdom on Judah's part will put both him and Tamar to the test.

The problem occurs when Judah does obey the law and gives his second son, Onan, to Tamar so that an heir can be produced to receive his dead brother's inheritance. However, Onan is greedy and does not wish to create competition for his share of Judah's property. He refuses to impregnate Tamar, and for this willful and foolish act God kills him (Gen. 38:9–10). Now Judah is left with only one more son, and he is naturally fearful for his son's life. Obviously, Tamar has proven herself to be an unlucky bride (compare with Sarah's plight in Tobit 3:7–9). As a result, Judah shames her by sending her back to her father's house and delaying indefinitely his sending his son to her to fulfill the family obligation (38:11).

Seeing that she will grow old before Judah again sends her one of his sons, Tamar steps out of the normal expectations of proper behavior. Knowing that Judah has recently become a widower, Tamar removes her widow's garments and replaces them with a provocative costume that identifies her as a prostitute. Then, as the patriarch travels with his flocks to Timnah to be sheared, he encounters her sitting alongside the road (38:14–15). It may be that he sees her as a sacred prostitute whose sexual favors are extended on behalf of a god of fertility—an aid to his efforts as a farmer and herdsman. Or, possibly, he is simply in need of female companionship after the death of his wife. In either case, Tamar's disguise, which includes a veil, fools Judah. He propositions her, haggles over the fee, and eventually takes his pleasure, leaving behind his seal and staff as surety for payment after the shearing (38:16–18).

Clothing and Social Expectation

Clothing marked a person's gender, social status, and availability for marriage, and it was a sign of power and wealth in ancient society. As with other customary or traditional behavior, the wearing of particular styles of clothing is also a sign of the acceptance of a social code. When a person sees someone else's costume, there is an immediate set of thoughts generated that governs proper response and expectations of behavior. Thus, Tamar's widow's garments are a graphic indication of who she is and what she ordinarily would be capable of doing within Israelite society. Similarly, Joseph's royal robes, when he becomes an adviser to the pharaoh, mask his Hebrew identity so thoroughly that even his brothers do not recognize him (Gen. 45:1–15).

The result of Tamar's deception is a pregnancy. She at last has the opportunity to fulfill her own obligation to her first husband by producing an heir for him. But she will also have to deal with the reaction to her apparently antisocial behavior. It is not surprising that Judah charges her with infidelity and condemns her to death. He had been looking for an excuse to remove her from his household, and she has now given him the perfect excuse. Nothing could be more fatal to women than evidence of adultery or promiscuity (see the accused bride in Deut. 22:13–21 and the adulterers in Deut. 22:22).

At this point in the story, the wisdom theme becomes clear. Tamar sends a private message to Judah telling him that the owner of the seal and staff that she now sends to him had impregnated her (38:25). Certainly, if she had wished to make a more dramatic revelation, she could have done this publicly. However, Tamar already has received what she wished from Judah, and she does not want to shame him before his own household. She shows great restraint and wisdom by knowing when to handle a situation in private. The result is Judah's acknowledgement that "she is more in the right than I" (38:26). Tamar has been able to transcend her identity as a powerless widow and demonstrate that some legal obligations are more important than strict adherence to one's usual role in society.

The story of another Tamar provides further evidence of the hard choices faced by the powerless. This Tamar is one of David's daughters and the full sister of David's son Absalom. She is forced to reason with her half-brother Amnon in an attempt to prevent him from raping her. Throughout the episode, Amnon is portrayed as a fool who cannot overcome his personal desires to take into account the rights or needs of others (2 Sam. 13:1–22). In that sense, he serves as a negative model within wisdom tradition as well as a violator of the laws protecting the weak from the strong in Israelite society.

Much of this narrative involves the political maneuvering that goes on in a royal household between the heirs to the throne. Tamar, in that sense, is merely a pawn used by both Amnon and her full brother Absalom to gain political advantage. The one person who might help her, her father David, actually adds fuel to the conflict between the brothers by sending Tamar to serve in Amnon's household to care for him in his pretended illness (13:7). Once he has her in his power, Amnon boldly demands that Tamar have sex with him (13:11). This in turn provides the background for a situation in which wisdom is her sole defense.

While the normal codes of correct behavior are sometimes bent or even violated by royalty (see David's adultery with Bathsheba in 2 Sam. 11:2–5), Tamar will use a wisdom argument to try to extricate herself from a damaging situation. Although she had no say in being sent to Amnon, Tamar now makes a very articulate defense of her honor. In doing so she also attempts to protect Amnon's honor from his baser desires, and thereby she becomes a champion for social morals and a true wisdom figure.

Because she cannot physically defend herself, Tamar relies upon a form of "shaming speech" to convince Amnon to think about his actions. Shaming, unlike curses and insults, is not an aggressive behavior. Instead, it serves as a rational social control mechanism. It employs a culturally based "vocabulary of embarrassment" to reason with potential lawbreakers or social deviants. The aim of shaming speech is to get the person to rethink his or her plans and to act honorably, not in the manner of fools who do not consider the consequences of their actions. Thus, Tamar responds to Amnon's proposition by saying, "No, my brother, do not force me; for such a thing is not done in Israel; do not do anything so vile!" (13:12).

Tamar's aim here is to draw on Amnon's sense of shame and to demonstrate to him that his impatience to assume David's throne does not have to include violating one of the "virgins of Israel." Her refusal to submit is the proper response, but it is not based on Israelite incest taboos. Instead, it is an argument for following the proper steps necessary to arrange and consummate a royal marriage. If he does not recognize the sense of her argument, he lays himself open to the charge of being a fool, a person who willingly violates the law (see the fate of the prodigal son in Deut. 21:18–21).

Her use of the label "fool" was intended to conjure up in his mind images of a person incapable of ruling either himself or the nation (see Prov. 11:29; 12:23; 26:1). The enemies are to be made fools of (Ex. 10:2; 1 Sam. 6:6), but it is not the label that a potential king would want next to his name. The Hebrew term used in this passage is often translated "scoundrel" (*nebalîm*). It is the same root as that of the name Nabal in 1 Samuel 25:2–22 and in both cases would have been used to describe men without principles or personal honor.

Finally, in desperation, Tamar asks Amnon to intercede with their father David so that a marriage can be arranged and they can be spared any public shame. Amnon has no intention, however, of submitting to David's lordship or letting him know how Amnon has misused Tamar. He is not concerned with doing the "honorable" thing. He is only interested in advancing his own political aims, and Tamar's violation is just one means he intends to use to weaken his brother Absalom's claim to the throne. In his own mind, Amnon believes that if he can take something away from Absalom without retaliation, he has proven himself a stronger candidate to become king. Both Tamar and the author of Proverbs agree that fools like Amnon "think their own way is right" (Prov. 12:15).

Whatever effect Tamar's shocking words were meant to have on her brother, they are not enough. He rapes her, and now Tamar is reduced to pleading that he marry her to cover her shame (2 Sam. 13:16). It is curious that she would even make the attempt after finding Amnon completely unresponsive to her previous wisdom argument. Still, it is the only way she has available to her to repair her social esteem and at least gain the honorable title of wife within her society. Again, however, Amnon has no intention of listening to her words. He has her physically removed from his house, and she is left, clothed in a torn robe and the ashes of mourning, to face a life without prospects of a royal marriage (13:17–19). Tamar's arguments mark her as a wisdom figure, but they do not preserve her from the reality of what is done to her.

Although personal tragedy such as this is a part of life, the laws of reciprocity still apply here. Amnon, the fool, cannot be allowed to get away with his violation of law and custom. Therefore, just as Nabal, the fool who dishonored David (1 Sam. 25), came to a bad end, Amnon also must pay the price for his abuse of the weak and his disregard for the wisdom arguments of Tamar. He is murdered by Absalom's men two years later, demonstrating that "fools die for lack of sense" (Prov. 10:21).

Wisdom Figures

To complete this examination of the wisdom theme, it is appropriate to single out certain biblical characters as wisdom figures. By their natural progression from "right thinking" to "right action," they set an example that can then serve as a model for others. It is certainly part of the wisdom theme's agenda to challenge the people to strive for improvement, if not perfection, and one way to do this is to provide them with paragons of wisdom. The wise teacher also hopes through words and illustrations to create wise students:

> The wise follow their teachers' advice, consequently their projects do not fail. ("Ptah-hotep," *OTP*, p. 269)

> Listen to what I say. Learn my words by heart…Live your lives with my words in your heart, and you will live your lives with success. ("Amen-em-ope," *OTP*, p. 275)

> Listen to advice and accept instruction, that you may gain wisdom for the future. (Prov. 19:20)

Solomon the Wise Ruler

One of the most natural choices for an idealized wisdom figure is King Solomon. He is portrayed in the official narrative as a thoughtful and just monarch. When given the chance to request divine assistance with his newly established administration, Solomon separates himself from common political leaders. Rather than ask for power, wealth, or the defeat of his enemies, he asks God for an "understanding mind to govern your people, able to discern between good and evil" (1 Kings 3:9). Whether this is more propaganda than reality, it still provides a goal for other rulers that stands in stark contrast to "Jeroboam's sin," a set of politically opportunistic acts used by the biblical writers as the measure of a bad or unjust king (see 1 Kings 12:25–33).

In fact, the biblical writers show their desire to portray Solomon's wisdom in the way they edited his royal annals. Instead of starting his chronicle with successful diplomatic efforts and major economic successes (both of which are in the annals), they start with the story of two prostitutes who come to Solomon for judgment (1 Kings 3:16–28). King David, Solomon's father, nearly came to political ruin because he failed on occasion to appoint judges or dispense justice himself (2 Sam. 15:2–6). This may have been in the minds of the editors, who wished to ensure that Solomon's reputation would be free from this charge of inefficiency.

As a result, these women who represent the lowest level of Israelite society are brought before the king, and he hears their case as if it were part of his normal daily routine. At issue is a child that each woman claims is her son. Another child has been accidentally smothered by his sleeping mother, and the two were sufficiently alike to cause confusion and allow an opportunistic woman to make a false claim (1 Kings 3:17–22). It is left to Solomon to discover the truth of the matter, and he does so by a psychological ploy. The king threatens to have the child cut in half so that each mother may have half of him. Naturally, the birth-mother does not wish to see her child killed and offers to give him up rather than see him die. This provides Solomon with the proof he needs to ascertain that the compassionate and self-sacrificing woman is indeed the true mother (3:23–27).

The point of the story is, therefore, to demonstrate Solomon's God-given wisdom and to prove that as Israel's new king he can discern truth and make the correct judgments necessary to bring prosperity to the land. In fact, the summary statement describing Solomon's rule is a reiteration and fulfillment of the covenant promise: "Judah and Israel were as numerous as the sand by the sea; they ate and drank and were happy" (1 Kings 4:20). Clearly, Solomon's willingness to humble himself before God and ask for wisdom sets him apart as a wise king, and thus his fame spreads throughout the earth.

The claim that his wisdom "surpassed the wisdom of all the people of the east, and all the wisdom of Egypt" (1 Kings 4:30) is a further expression of the universalism theme. It brings visitors from other lands to hear this teacher (4:34), including the queen of Sheba (10:1–10). As a true seeker of wisdom, she comes to test Solomon, but at the same time to test his God. When Solomon is able to answer all her questions, this non-Israelite monarch proclaims her faith in the king's true wisdom and also makes a statement praising Yahweh, "who has delighted in you and set you on the throne of Israel" (10:9). In this way, Solomon's international reputation is affirmed, and the sense of Yahweh's universal power is advanced.

The Perfect Wife of Proverbs

The book of Proverbs contains contrasting examples of chaste and promiscuous women. A strange woman entices "young men without sense" off the street to enter her rooms and commit adulterous acts as she leads them to ultimate destruction (7:7–9). She is portrayed as a harlot, "wily of heart," who seduces him with kisses and assurances that only he is the object of her affections. Her perfumed bed awaits their pleasure while her husband is away on a long journey (7:16–20). In contrast, "Dame Wisdom" sends her servants into the street to gather the "simple" and those "without sense" to come to her table to eat and drink from her teachings that will bring them maturity and an insightful life (9:1–6).

Drawing on this model of female wisdom is the **acrostic** poem (in Hebrew) at the end of Proverbs 31 that lays out the qualities of the idealized wife. It seems likely that this final portion of the book provides an opportunity to summarize and reiterate the qualities of a wise woman and the blessings achieved by her household that are found in Proverbs 1–9:

Female Wisdom:

- Hear, my child, your father's instruction, and do not reject your mother's teaching. (1:8)
- She opens her mouth with wisdom, and the teaching of kindness is on her tongue. (31:26)

Value of Dame Wisdom:

- She is more precious than jewels, and nothing you desire can compare with her. (3:15)
- A capable wife who can find? She is far more precious than jewels. (31:10)

This paragon of domestic virtue is said to have all the necessary abilities to manage a household. She is able to wisely choose the best grades of wool and flax for her weaving and to organize family meals, bringing together the necessary items from the family larder and from the market. To accomplish these tasks efficiently, this perfect wife rises early to begin the day's chores and to assign tasks to the servants (31:13–15).

The text then adds a dimension that is not usually found in the description of women: business transactions (31:16). Ordinarily, women did not have the legal standing to purchase land, although they certainly worked hard with their families to cultivate it and deal with its produce. Still, there is in this verse and in the ones that describe her weaving (31:19–22) a sense of intense activity performed by a determined woman willing to "gird up her loins" (i.e., push up her sleeves). All this is to say that she brings order and prosperity to her household (compare with Prov. 3:14 and 8:21), ensuring that her family is well-clothed in fine garments and in the honest virtues of the wise. To have her husband, her children, and her neighbors bless her is the highest goal for a mother in the covenant community (31:28–31).

Conclusion

This final section dealing with the benefits derived from obedience to the covenant and from a life striving for wisdom is an appropriate ending for this volume. Throughout the discussion in each chapter it becomes clear that these four major biblical themes (covenant, remnant, universalism, and wisdom) complement each other. It is impossible to be wise if one is not faithful to the covenant obligations. There is no possibility that a person will be among the righteous remnant if he or she has not had the wisdom to "fear God" and thus have the knowledge necessary to survive the calamities that God brings upon the unfaithful. And, finally, the development of Israelite religion out of a polytheistic environment, through the middle ground of henotheism and the dangers of **syncretism** (borrowing from other cultures), to monotheism is an expression of a more mature understanding of the covenant. It reflects an acknowledgment of the universal and transcendent powers of Yahweh and a total rejection of all other gods.

Glossary

acrostic: literary device in which each line/stanza begins with a consecutive letter of the alphabet.

annunciation: a birth announcement made by God or a divine representative.

apodictic: a type of legal statement which is in the form of a command, without explanation.

ark of the covenant: the gold-covered box created to house the Ten Commandments. It was carried by the Levites and was kept in the Holy of Holies of the tabernacle during the wilderness period.

assimilation: a set of actions designed to transform a stranger into a member of a group.

call narrative: the event in which a person is called to become a prophet.

canon: those books designated by the faith community as holy scripture and the standard for faith and practice.

city-state: a political unit composed of an urban center and its immediate environs and villages.

concubine: a secondary wife who has not been able to provide a dowry. Her children may not inherit from their father's property unless he officially designates them as heirs.

corporate responsibility: a legal principle that rewards or punishes an entire household for the righteousness or the sins of the head of the household.

covenant: the contractual agreement between Yahweh and the chosen people that promises land and children in exchange for exclusive worship and obedience.

Covenant Code: this earliest of the biblical law codes includes Exodus 20:18–23:33 and represents the society of the early monarchy period.

covenant renewal ceremony: a ritual used several times by Israelite leaders to reinforce the importance of the covenant with Yahweh.

culling process: the method of eliminating the unfaithful during the wilderness period.

cultic: anything having to do with religious activity.

Decalogue: the Ten Commandments.

demythologize: the process of using elements of a myth from another culture without ascribing any powers to the gods in those stories.

Deuterocanon or **Apocrypha**: the books (1 and 2 Macc., Jdt., etc.) written between 300 B.C.E.–100 B.C.E. that are contained in the Septuagint and the Vulgate, and are accepted by Roman Catholics but not by Protestants and Jews.

Deuteronomic Code: this biblical law code dates to the late monarchic period and comprises Deuteronomy 12–26.

diasporic community/diaspora: the body of Israelite people taken into the exile and those who chose to remain in these foreign lands.

disqualification stories: a set of stories designed to eliminate a person or a family from succession to the throne of Israel or from inheriting the covenantal promise.

divine assembly: the divine company that serves as a decision-making body in ancient Near Eastern religion. In Israelite belief, Yahweh's divine assembly act as messengers and are portrayed surrounding enthroned Yahweh.

divine warrior: the role of Yahweh in warfare on behalf of the Israelites.

diviner: one who used ritual methods to determine the will of the gods.

egalitarian: a social system in which all persons have equal status under the law.

enacted prophecy: a prophecy that includes an action, physical or symbolic, by the prophet that is designed to draw attention and to reinforce the message.

endogamy: a policy of marrying only within a certain, identifiable group.

etiological: a story that is designed to explain the origin of a event, the background of a place name, or the basis for a tradition.

genre: a category of literature (i.e., short story, poetry).

henotheism: the belief in the existence of many gods, but the choice to worship only one.

herem: a type of "holy war" in which conquered people and all their possessions are destroyed as a sacrifice to God.

hesed: "everlasting love"—a covenantal term that is used as the basis for Yahweh's willingness to make a covenant with the people.

Holiness Code: the last of the biblical legal codes to be developed (ca. 500 B.C.E.). This code, which is primarily concerned with ritual purity, is found in Leviticus 17–26.

Jeroboam's sin: the actions taken by king Jeroboam I (1 Kings 12:25–33) to establish a separate identity for the Northern Kingdom. They were used by the biblical writers as the hallmark of the "evil king."

lament: a form of writing found principally in the Psalms that recounts sorrow or suffering by an individual or a group.

legend: a story that centers on human heroes or founders of nations and includes superhuman feats or dealings with gods.

levirate obligation: a legal method to provide an heir for a man who dies before fathering children. His nearest male kin is required to impregnate the widow (see Deut. 25:5–10).

liminal: a person who stands on the threshold between one society or one social status and another. Because the person does not fit into a regular category, he or she is free to transcend the normal rules of society.

liturgy: the outline and stages of a worship service.

messiah: the Hebrew word for "anointed," used for those individuals chosen by Yahweh for leadership positions.

motif: a repeated story line in a narrative.

oracle: a prophetic speech.

pantheon: all the gods in a religious system.

proselytes: converts to a faith community.

remnant: the portion of the community who will, according to the prophets, survive God's wrath and rebuild the nation.

ritual purity: the steps taken to transform persons or objects into a "clean" or "pure" religious state.

Sabbath: the celebration of Yahweh as the creator God and the commemoration of the creation event by ceasing work one day each week.

sackcloth: a roughly woven garment worn as a sign of mourning or repentance.

Shema: the statement of faith of the Israelites found in Deuteronomy 6:4.

syncretism: the borrowing of cultural ideas and traits from neighboring peoples.

theodicy: an explanation for God's actions, most often found in the words of the prophets.

theogony: a story describing the origins of the gods.

theophany: the appearance of God to a human being.

transcendent: a characteristic of a deity who is separate from the creation and is not affected by the forces of nature.

universalism: a theme in the biblical narrative that attempts to demonstrate that Yahweh is a universal god by having a non-Israelite make a statement of faith or remark about Yahweh's power.

wisdom (literature): a type of literature that concentrates on the basic values and common sense of a culture.

Yahweh: one of the names for the Israelite God in the Bible, which is sometimes anglicized into Jehovah. It is associated with the J-source. In the English translation of the Bible, Yahweh is always translated "Lord."

Zion: the hill within Jerusalem where Solomon constructed the temple to Yahweh. In later tradition it became synonymous with Jerusalem and the hope of return.

Select Bibliography

Ancient Near Eastern Texts

Lambert, W. G. *Babylonian Wisdom Literature.* Oxford: Clarendon Press, 1960.

Matthews, V. H., and D. C. Benjamin. *Old Testament Parallels: Laws and Stories from the Ancient Near East*, 2d ed. Mahwah, N.J.: Paulist Press, 1997.

Pritchard, J. *Ancient Near Eastern Texts Relating to the Old Testament*, 3d ed. Princeton, N.J.: Princeton University Press, 1969.

Roth, M. T. *Law Collections from Mesopotamia and Asia Minor.* Atlanta: Scholars Press, 1995.

Social World of the Ancient Near East

Aberbach, M. *Labor, Crafts and Commerce in Ancient Israel.* Jerusalem: Magnes, 1994.

Borowski, O. *Agriculture in Iron Age Israel.* Winona Lake, Ind.: Eisenbrauns, 1987.

DeVries, L. F. *Cities of the Biblical World.* Peabody, Mass.: Hendrickson, 1997.

Matthews, V. H. *Manners and Customs in the Bible*, rev. ed. Peabody, Mass.: Hendrickson, 1991.

——, and D. C. Benjamin. *Social World of Ancient Israel 1250–587 B.C.E.* Peabody, Mass.: Hendrickson, 1993.

Snell, D. C. *Life in the Ancient Near East.* New Haven, Conn.: Yale University Press, 1997.

History of the Ancient Near East

Jacobsen, T. *The Treasures of Darkness: A History of Mesopotamian Religion.* New Haven, Conn.: Yale University Press, 1976.

James, T. G. H. *Pharaoh's People.* Chicago: University of Chicago Press, 1984.

Knapp, A. B. *The History and Culture of Ancient Western Asia and Egypt.* Chicago: Dorsey Press, 1988.

Miller, J. M., and J. H. Hayes. *A History of Ancient Israel and Judah.* Philadelphia: Westminster Press, 1986.

Redford, D. B. *Egypt, Canaan, and Israel in Ancient Times.* Princeton, N.J.: Princeton University Press, 1992.

Covenant

Brueggemann, W. *The Covenanted Self: Explorations in Law and Covenant.* Minneapolis: Fortress Press, 1999.

Hillers, D. R. *Covenant: The History of a Biblical Idea.* Baltimore: Johns Hopkins University Press, 1969.

McCarthy, D. *Old Testament Covenant: A Survey of Current Opinions.* Richmond,Va.: John Knox, 1972.

Mendenhall, G. *The Tenth Generation.* Baltimore: Johns Hopkins University Press, 1973.

———, and G. A. Herion. "Covenant." In *Anchor Bible Dictionary*, vol. 1, 1179–1202. New York: Doubleday, 1992.

Nicholson, E. W. *God and His People: Covenant Theology in the Old Testament.* Oxford: Clarendon Press, 1986.

Sakenfeld, K. D. *The Meaning of Hesed in the Hebrew Bible: A New Inquiry.* Missoula, Mont.: Scholars Press, 1978.

Viberg, A. *Symbols of Law.* Stockholm: Almqvist & Wiksell, 1992.

Remnant

Hasel, G. F. *The Remnant: The History and Theology of the Remnant Idea from Genesis to Isaiah.* Berrien Springs, Mich.: Andrews University Press, 1972.

Hubbard, D. A. "Hope in the Old Testament," *Tyndale Bulletin* 34 (1983): 33–59.

Peckham, B. *History and Prophecy: the Development of Late Judean Literary Traditions.* New York: Doubleday, 1993.

Widengren, G. "Yahweh's Gathering of the Dispersed." In *In the Shelter of Elyon.* Edited by W. Barrick and J. Spencer, 227–45. Sheffield: Sheffield University Press, 1984.

Universalism

Batto, B. F. *Slaying the Dragon: Mythmaking in the Biblical Tradition.* Louisville, Ky.: Westminster/John Knox Press, 1992.

Blenkinsopp, J. "Second Isaiah—A Prophet of Universalism," *Journal for the Study of the Old Testament* 41 (1988): 83–103.

Cross, F. M. *Canaanite Myth and Hebrew Epic.* Cambridge, Mass.: Harvard University Press, 1971.

Dearman, J. A. *Religion and Culture in Ancient Israel.* Peabody, Mass.: Hendrickson, 1992.

Gray, J. *I & II Kings: A Commentary.* Philadelphia: Westminster, 1970.

Wisdom

Crenshaw, J. L. *Education in Ancient Israel.* New York: Doubleday, 1998.
———. *Old Testament Wisdom: An Introduction.* 2d ed. Louisville, Ky.: Westminster John Knox Press, 1999.
Gammie, J., and L. G. Perdue, eds. *The Sage in Israel and the Ancient Near East.* Winona Lake, Ind.: Eisenbrauns, 1990.
McKane, W. *Proverbs: a New Approach.* Philadelphia: Westminster, 1970.
Matthews, V. H. "Female Voices: Upholding the Honor of the Household," *Biblical Theology Bulletin* 24 (1994): 8–15.
Murphy, R. E. *Proverbs.* Word Biblical Commentary, 22. Nashville: Thomas Nelson, 1998.

Subject Index

Scripture Index